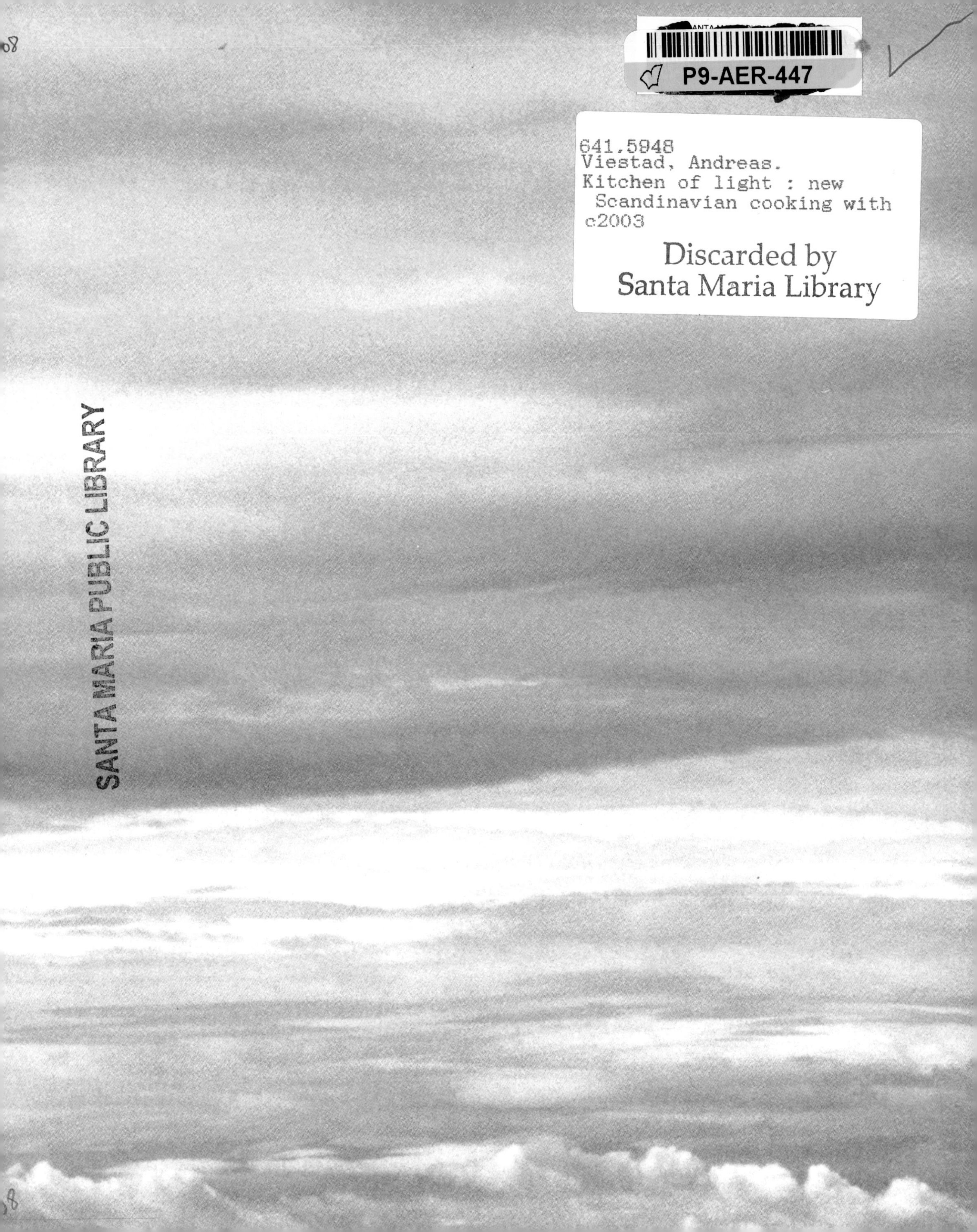

kit-
chen
of
light

kit-chen of light

NEW SCANDINAVIAN COOKING WITH

ANDREAS VIESTAD

PHOTOGRAPHS BY METTE RANDEM

ARTISAN

NEW YORK

To my grandmother, Inga Johnsen,
for all she has given—and continues to give

Contents

INTRODUCTION

Today I woke up to a new light.

Yesterday was cold and dark here in Oslo, with clear signs that autumn was losing out to the inevitability of winter. One week ago a determined wind from the north had decided to swipe all the yellow and red leaves off the trees, and once the street cleaners had done their job, grayness seemed to engulf everything but the brightly colored buildings in the center of the city.

Then today was a new day. When I pulled the curtains aside, expecting just another bleak Sunday morning, I found that the world outside had been transformed. A white blanket of snow covered the streets, trees, and rooftops, turning the busy capital into a chaotic fairy-tale city with skidding cars and joyful children at play. And, although the sun has long since withdrawn from the energetic omnipresence of summer, the day is bright in a way only a winter day in the high north can be.

Norway lies about as far north as is humanly habitable. The climate and nature are at times extreme. In northern Norway the sun never sets during the summer months, and during the long winter it never rises above the horizon. The south coast of the country, considered a summer holiday paradise by many Norwegians, is on the same latitude as southern Alaska.

While this territory makes hard demands, it is also generous. Norway has a long coastline with some of the world's richest fisheries, making fish and seafood a cornerstone of Scandinavian cooking. As the country is sparsely populated, most of nature is unspoiled, allowing for plenty of game and lamb to roam the countryside freely. Norway's long summer days provide fruits and vegetables with an intensity of flavor that makes us believe they are the best in the world.

Fishing and gathering are still important in everyday life. Even Oslo, a modern Norwegian city with its share of stress, skyscrapers, traffic jams, and dot com companies, is surrounded by the sea on one side and the forest—abundant with porcini, chanterelles, game, and berries—on the other. Every day people fish for salmon and crayfish from the piers outside City Hall. My father, who lives fifteen minutes from the city center, is often visited by moose in his garden. Travel twenty minutes north or south of the city and you can enjoy nature at its most beautiful.

As you might imagine, living in Scandinavia means having a close and important relationship with nature, especially in regard to food. Until recently, Scandinavian cooking was simply home cooking, "food" but not "cuisine." Today, Scandinavian food is something quite different. Norwegian chefs and restaurants are held in a high international esteem. Oslo has one Michelin star for every seventy thousand inhabitants, which is among the highest star-density for any capital, and Norwegian chefs have won the unofficial world championship in cooking—the Bocuse d'Or—several times.

However, after a decade of experimenting with fusion and crossover cooking, Scandinavians are now returning to the basics. While modern Scandinavian cooking can be dazzling and extravagant, it is more about appealing to our basic appetites and need to eat. With its elegant and simple cooking and its emphasis on fresh, natural ingredients, modern Scandinavian cooking is to northern Europe what Provençal and Tuscan cuisines are to the south. Regional specialties—like gravlaks, cod, and smorgasbord—have been rediscovered and refined. Once again, Scandinavians are taking pride in their food traditions and the superb ingredients our homeland has to offer: good meat, simple and tasty vegetables, some

of the best fish in the world, and oh-so-sweet fruits and berries.

Scandinavia consists of more than just my native Norway. To the south is Denmark, with rich food traditions that sometimes differ considerably from those of the rest of Scandinavia, and to the east is Sweden, with a similar cuisine but with many local variations. You will find that most of the recipes in this book are of Norwegian origin, but a significant number are from Denmark or Sweden, and since the relationships among our countries are so close, historically, culturally, and culinarily, there are quite a few recipes of genuinely pan-Scandinavian origin.

As a home cook in the United States, you will find that most of the ingredients in my recipes are easy to find and the cooking techniques are relatively simple. A large portion of this book was written while I was living in Boston, and the food has been adapted to ingredients that I could obtain in local shops there. There are a few Scandinavian specialties that may be harder to find, but they are too important to leave out and worth the search. In these cases I have included a list of mail-order sources (page 294) and, where applicable, I have suggested substitutes that will leave you with delicious food nonetheless.

Kitchen of Light is a book about food and the offerings of the table. It is the companion book to my public television series, *New Scandinavian Cooking with Andreas Viestad*. You may recognize that many of the people and much of the food I write about were featured on the show. Writing the book and making the television series simultaneously have been intense and demanding, but, most of all, they have been inspiring and rewarding.

While I am passionate about food, I am not a chef. I cook because I am hungry and because I am inspired by the offerings that each season brings: the ecstasy of long summer days when all you have to do for dinner is bring a bucket down to the shore and fill it with mussels and pick berries that have been sweetened by a sun that never sets; the softness of autumn's growing shadows—the richest time of year—with game, apples, honey, and golden chanterelles agleam in the forest;

the white and blue light of winter, with nights when warm soups and rich meat dishes promise the comfort and warmth of family life; and then, coming full circle, we welcome the joyful ardor of the sun in early spring, signaling a return to life, with the spawning cod and the first coming of migratory birds—an awakening of the senses.

Kitchen of Light is part cookbook, part introduction to a region, and part story about my family, friends, and the food we share. May it inspire you to embrace new flavors.

1

ON THE WINGS OF FORTUNE

I have never thought of myself as someone who would thrive in extreme conditions—I am just too comfortable being comfortable—but driving sixty miles an hour across the vast icy expanses of Spitsbergen on a snow-mobile, completely covered, almost mummified, in multiple layers of wool undergarments and windproof winter wear, I feel like the king of the Arctic. I find myself imagining that I am a cowboy and my snowmobile is my horse. But then I remember that there is no need to use my imagination— the place where I am is really more dangerous and exotic than even the most faraway prairie or desert. I am having the experience of a lifetime.

I have come here to tape an episode of my television series, *New Scandinavian Cooking.* This is the last frontier, the northernmost Norwegian territory and one of the few remaining areas of totally unspoiled wilderness in Europe, even the world. Out here there is nothing but snow, ice, and the occasional polar bear. If we get stranded, we will definitely not last long.

While mainland Norway can at times seem rough and inhospitable, like living near the margins of existence, Spitsbergen, a barren and beautiful island in the Svalbard archipelago, less than 750 miles from the North Pole, is far more extreme. Most of the year the island is covered by a blanket of snow and ice, and it is shrouded in darkness for more than four months each winter. It is impossible to grow anything here—a few robust shrubs, lichen, moss, and some fragile flowers are the only vegetation that can be found during the bright, cool summer. At a latitude of 79 degrees north, it is the northernmost inhabited place in the world, and the twenty-five hundred inhabitants who live here could not survive without the help of technology and a steady supply of goods from the mainland. On the outskirts of Longyearbyen

("Longyear City," named after its American discoverer, John Monroe Longyear), the capital of the Svalbard archipelago, a "Beware of the Polar Bear" sign reminds us that we are only visitors here, that this territory really belongs to nature.

My guide is Ann Jorid Pedersen, a woman in her thirties who says she got the Svalbard bug after her first visit in the 1980s, and

who ten years later gave up a comfortable life on the mainland in order to live in the Arctic.

In her office in Longyearbyen, she is a modern businesswoman who deals with travel agents and tourists from all over the world. But when she is wrapped in her sealskin jacket and furry hat, she looks like one of the gatherers

who used to live here, and seeing the way she drives her snowmobile, and her confident way of handling the rifle she carries to protect us from attacking polar bears, makes it hard to believe that she is not native to this wilderness.

Now, in early May, life is as good as it gets at this latitude. Winter and summer have collided in a spectacular show of force: The landscape is as icy and wintry white as ever, but at the same time the midnight sun shines all day and all night. It is a bit on the cool side, I must admit—around zero degrees—and whenever I stop the snowmobile and pull off one of the three hats I'm wearing, so I can enjoy the intense quiet of the Arctic, my ears start to burn with the cold. But once wrapped up again I feel protected and warm, and the beauty of nature and the intensity of the light more than make up for the cold.

Svalbard is home to large colonies of seals and walruses, polar bears, and a special subspecies of reindeer not found anywhere else in the world. The reindeer are highly adapted to life on Svalbard: Furry, short-legged, and heavily built, they have a thick layer of body fat that protects them against the cold, allowing them to survive for long periods of time without food. The islands have visitors as well: Every spring, flocks of geese arrive from southern Europe and Africa to nest and to feed on the little vegetation there is. Seeing the elegant long-necked geese arriving, quacking happily as they fly into the icy valleys, you wonder how they can possibly fit into this environment, but they do, and during the short summer they grow surprisingly fat.

We are traveling from Long-yearbyen to the Temple Fjord at the foot of the Von Post Glacier, where MS *Origo,* a small cruise ship that has been left to freeze in the ice, serves as a hotel. We have the best weather possible, with clear blue skies and an unlimited view. Then suddenly, just as we catch a glimpse of the boat in the distance, the weather changes, and within five minutes we are engulfed by a ferocious snowstorm. We have to reduce speed, and even though I am driving less than a hundred feet behind Ann's snowmobile, I sometimes lose sight of her red taillights.

When we finally arrive at the ship, I feel frozen, more like the frail city boy I am than the adventurer that I had earlier imagined. Later in the evening, after we have thawed out, we make supper—a beet soup inspired by the Russian borscht, but using goose stock from the local Svalbard geese instead of beef stock.

While the goose and beet soup is cooking, filling the ship with a maddeningly delicious smell, I read a book about the trappers and hunters who lived on Svalbard more than a century ago. They all wrote diaries to maintain their sanity and keep track of time.

Confined as they were most of the time inside their small cabins, food seemed to be the only thing that really interested them, and their diaries are full of longing for fresh food, as well as complaints about rancid meat and insufficient provisions. Only two things were able to lighten their gloomy moods: the occasional chocolate from the small supply they brought with them from the mainland and the springtime arrival of geese. Eating the rich goose meat after months of seal meat and oat porridge filled them with bliss. "Today we had roast goose, flown in from the Nubia on the wings of fortune," one hunter wrote ecstatically.

The Svalbard goose has all the luxurious complexity of farmed goose, but also a rich gamy flavor that only the special combination of tropical and Arctic vegetation can provide.

That night, safe in the belly of the ship as the snowstorm raged outside, I felt truly blessed. Eating the simple steaming hot soup in the small teak-lined dining room was one of the most enjoyable dining experiences I have ever had.

THIS IS A HIGH NORTH VERSION OF THE RUSSIAN BEET SOUP BORSCHT. THE SWEET AND AROMATIC GOOSE STOCK MAKES IT SLIGHTLY MORE SOPHISTICATED THAN THE HEARTY RUSSIAN VERSIONS.

THE FIRST TIME I MADE IT WAS IN SVALBARD, AN ARCHIPELAGO HALFWAY BETWEEN MAINLAND NORWAY AND THE NORTH POLE. STOCK FROM WILD SVALBARD GOOSE ADDED A RICH GAMY QUALITY. STOCK FROM FARM-RAISED GOOSE HAS A MILDER FLAVOR.

Svalbard Beet Soup with Goose Stock

SERVES 4

2 tablespoons olive oil

2 red onions, chopped

2 garlic cloves, finely chopped

2 pounds beets, peeled and cut into 1-inch dice

2 bay leaves

2 carrots, chopped

5 cups Goose Stock or Duck Stock (recipe follows)

1 teaspoon chili powder, or more to taste

2 to 3 tablespoons fresh lemon juice

Fine sea salt and freshly ground black pepper

¼ cup sour cream or yogurt

In a medium pot, heat the oil over medium heat. Sauté the onions and garlic until soft and light brown, 4 to 5 minutes. Add the beets, bay leaves, carrots, and stock and bring to a boil. Reduce the heat and simmer for 35 to 40 minutes, until the beets are soft. Remove the bay leaves. Transfer the soup to a blender, in batches if necessary, and puree until smooth.

Return the soup to the pot and reheat. Season with the chili powder, lemon juice, and salt and pepper.

Pour the soup into bowls. Add a tablespoon of sour cream to each bowl, and serve.

Goose and duck meat may be delicious, but most of the flavor lies hidden in the bones. Cooking leftover bones and meat in water with aromatic vegetables is a simple thing, yet the stock you get is rich and delicious. You can also use this recipe for turkey or chicken, making a somewhat lighter stock.

The stock can be frozen for up to 2 months.

Goose or Duck Stock   MAKES 6 TO 7 CUPS

1 tablespoon unsalted butter

1 onion, chopped

2 quarts cold water

2 pounds goose, duck, or turkey bones, coarsely chopped

4 carrots, chopped

1 cup chopped celeriac

2 bay leaves

Heat the butter in a large pot over medium heat. Add the onion and sauté for 5 minutes, or until soft and golden. Add the water, goose bones, carrots, celeriac, and bay leaves and bring to a boil; with a large spoon, skim off the foam that forms on the surface. Reduce the heat and simmer gently for 1 hour and 15 minutes.

Line a colander or sieve with cheesecloth and strain the stock into a bowl or other container. Cover and refrigerate until ready to use.

Traditional Vegetable Beef Soup

SERVES 6

2 pounds beef neck or another tough cut, excess fat removed, cut into ½-inch chunks

1 large celeriac, peeled and cut into ½-inch chunks

1 onion, cut into ⅓-inch slices

3 to 4 carrots, cut into ½-inch slices

2 leeks, white and pale green parts only, washed and cut into 1-inch pieces

10 black peppercorns

2 bay leaves

2 quarts water

Fine sea salt

2 tablespoons chopped fresh herbs, such as parsley, sage, and thyme, for garnish

2 teaspoons grated orange or lemon zest for garnish (optional)

Place the meat, celeriac, onion, half the carrots, half the leeks, the peppercorns, and bay leaves in a large pot. Add the water, bring to a boil, and with a large spoon, skim off the foam that forms on the surface. Reduce the heat and let the soup simmer gently for 2 hours.

Add the remaining carrots and leeks and simmer for 8 more minutes, or until tender. Season with salt to taste.

Pour the soup into bowls, garnish with the fresh herbs and orange zest, if using, and serve.

Duck Soup with Madeira

SERVES 4

IF YOU DO NOT WANT TO MAKE YOUR OWN STOCK FOR THIS RECIPE, YOU CAN SUBSTITUTE COMMERCIAL DUCK STOCK.

6 cups Duck Stock (page 18) or 4 cups chicken stock plus 2 cups beef stock

2 cups heavy (whipping) cream

¼ cup sweet Madeira or sweet sherry

1 carrot, finely chopped

¼ cup finely chopped fennel

¼ cup finely chopped leek, white and pale green parts only

1 pound cooked duck or chicken, chopped (optional)

1 tablespoon finely chopped fresh sage

¼ cup chopped sugar snap peas

Fine sea salt and freshly ground black pepper

Bring the stock to a boil in a large pot over medium heat. Stir in the cream and Madeira. Add the carrot, fennel, leek, and duck, if using, and bring to a simmer. Reduce the heat to medium-low and simmer for 5 minutes.

Add the sage and snap peas and season with salt and pepper. Pour into bowls and serve.

Sweet Madeira wine has been known in Norway for centuries—originally it was bartered for dried salt cod. It gives a wonderful flavor to duck or goose stock.

Serve the soup with good crusty bread to sop up all the broth.

FISH SOUP: THE BERGEN REMEDY

To me, the only remedy for long rainy days is soup. The warm comfort of a good filling fish soup is one of the few things that can make up for the lack of sun. The people of Bergen, Norway's second largest city, need that remedy more often than most. Situated at the end of a fjord, the city, known to most Norwegians as "the Rainy City," is trapped between seven ragged mountains. Warm, humid air from the Atlantic Ocean is blown into the fjord by the more or less constant westerly wind and then trapped by the cold mountains, causing rain more than 260 days a year. People dress appropriately, but a raincoat or umbrella is seldom far away. You will find strategically located umbrella-vending machines in and around town.

But despite the gray skies and the more or less constant dampness, it is still said that Bergen has the highest quality of life and the most content population in Norway. Whereas Oslo, the capital, is a modern city with a constantly changing cityscape and population, Bergen has maintained a nineteenth-century grandeur, a self-contented Old World atmosphere that strangers sometimes interpret—rightly or wrongly—as arrogance. The industrial base has changed considerably since the time when cod was king and sailing ships from Bergen were found in ports all over the world. Today academia, shipbuilding, and hypermodern fish farming are the most important industries, but through its stubborn and proud city patriotism, Bergen has managed to make the transformation to modernity without losing its soul.

Nowhere are that pride and soul more visible than at the fish market in the middle of town. In the square next to the long rectangular harbor lies northern Europe's largest outdoor fish market, with dozens of stalls offering a huge selection of the freshest fish and shellfish. Despite the rain, the market is always crowded with people, and on Saturdays there are long lines. Walking through the market can make even the most ardent carnivore develop a deep hunger for fish, and even though I am always there as a visitor and hardly ever have access to kitchen facilities, I can walk around the market for hours, enjoying the atmosphere and imagining what I would prepare. There are scary-looking monkfish with their enormous heads and monsterlike faces, shiny green and blue mackerel, beautiful pink salmon, sad-eyed redfish, fierce-looking wolffish, enormous halibut, charmingly freckled plaice, and the occasional mackerel shark. There is also an abundance of fish roe products, and smoked salmon with an orange tint, which tells you that the fish has been smoked in an old-fashioned smokehouse. You can even buy live fish: A few of the best stalls have giant saltwater tanks filled with live crabs, lobsters, pollock, or cod. With most fish, freshness is of utmost importance, and nothing could be a better quality assurance than to see your dinner swimming around in clear water just hours before you cook it.

When I get hungry from looking at all the fish, I buy an oyster, shucked by the fishmonger and offered in the half-shell, or a freshly boiled Norwegian lobster—a small, pale orange, crawfishlike crustacean with pink sweet lobster-flavored flesh, one of the finest foods I know. It needs nothing to complement it, and I eat it with my hands as I walk.

The fabulous access to fresh fish has left its mark on both the city and its cooking. While Norway as a whole has experienced an often troubling internationalization of its everyday cooking, in Bergen, traditional food is still a part of the everyday diet and people have access to plenty of good, cheap local food. Workers can choose between international foods such as kebabs and hamburgers or traditional smoked salmon sandwiches and fish soup for lunch—the price is more or less the same. There is even a fish-based fast-food shop near the city square where the Hagelin sisters sell snow-white fish dumplings and other traditional dishes.

Bergen's most important contribution to international cuisine is its fish soup, which, according to many, deserves a place alongside bouillabaisse as one of the best fish soups in the world. The soup is the extreme opposite of its French counterpart: Where the sun-scorched bouillabaisse is temperamental and pushy, Bergen fish soup is warming and seductive. The soup is made with stock from young pollock, and the orthodox will tell you that the pollock must be bought live at the fish market the same day you make the soup, but I have found that it tastes just as good with fish stock from the fishmonger. With no herbs or spices for flavor, just root vegetables, the soup is totally dependent on the quality of the fish. The addition of sugar and sour cream, and sometimes a few drops of vinegar, gives it an interesting sweet-and-sour flavor, but apart from that, the soup is just the refined essence of the sea, with a purity and flavor-richness unsurpassed by any other fish soup I have tasted.

WHILE THE CLASSIC WAY TO MAKE THIS
FISH SOUP IS WITH YOUR OWN STOCK
MADE FROM VERY FRESH YOUNG POLLOCK,
IT IS ABSOLUTELY PERMISSIBLE TO USE
FISH STOCK BOUGHT FROM THE LOCAL
FISHMONGER.

Bergen Fish Soup

SERVES 10

There are different, equally authentic ways of making the soup. The big schism is between those who like to thicken the soup with a combination of flour and cream, so it becomes like a chowder, and those who prefer it thin. I think it is easier to appreciate the unique sweet-and-sour freshness of the soup when it is made with only the minimum of thickener.

Its combined lightness and richness make it easy to eat a lot of the fish soup, but any leftovers can be frozen for later.

3 quarts fish stock (see headnote)

4 carrots, cut into 1-inch by $1/4$-inch sticks

I large celeriac, peeled and cut into 1-inch by $1/4$-inch sticks

2 small parsley roots or parsnips, peeled and cut into 1-inch by $1/4$-inch sticks

2 celery stalks, chopped

1 to 2 tablespoons all-purpose flour for thickening (optional)

1 cup heavy (whipping) cream

2 tablespoons sugar

$1/4$ cup good red wine vinegar, or to taste

$1/2$ cup salted veal stock (optional)

Fine sea salt

$1 1/2$ pounds mixed fish fillets, such as salmon, cod, and halibut, or other firm white-fleshed fish, cut into 2-inch chunks

Fish Dumplings (recipe follows)

3 large egg yolks

One 8-ounce container sour cream

Chopped fresh chives for garnish (optional)

Bring the fish stock to a boil in a large pot. Add the vegetables, reduce the heat, and let simmer for 5 minutes.

If you are using the flour, whisk it together with the cream in a small bowl, add the cream to the soup, and bring to a boil. Add the sugar and vinegar to taste; the soup should have a subtle sweet-and-sour flavor. Add the veal stock, if using, and salt to taste. Add the fish and fish dumplings, bring to a boil, reduce the heat, and simmer for 7 to 8 minutes, until the fish is just cooked.

In the meantime, whisk together the egg yolks and sour cream in a small bowl. Pour the soup into bowls, dividing the fish and dumplings evenly. Gently stir 2 to 3 tablespoons of the sour cream mixture into each bowl. Sprinkle with chives, if desired, and serve.

Fish Dumplings

1 pound cod fillet, skin and bones removed

2 large eggs

2 to 3 tablespoons cornstarch

1 teaspoon fine sea salt

1½ teaspoons freshly ground white pepper

2 cups whipped cream

Run the fish through a meat grinder twice; it should be very fine and smooth. (You can also use a food processor, although it can be more difficult to get a smooth consistency that way.)

In a large bowl, lightly beat the eggs. Add the cornstarch, salt, pepper, and fish and mix well. Gently fold the cream into the fish mixture, trying not to deflate cream.

With a spoon, form the dumpling mixture into small balls.

NOTE: If serving the dumplings on their own, bring a pot of salted water (or fish stock) to a boil. Add the dumplings, reduce the heat, and simmer for about 7 minutes, until cooked through. Remove with a slotted spoon, and serve with béchamel sauce, if desired.

Homemade fish dumplings are an important part of Bergen fish soup. The goal is to make them as light as possible. The dumplings can also be served on their own, or with a dill-flavored béchamel.

Spinach Soup with Tarragon-Poached Eggs

SERVES 4

This is a modernized version of the traditional nettle soup that in Norway marks the coming of spring. Picking nettles, even the young ones used in the soup, can be painful, so when I found out that the soup tasted just as good with spinach, I was thoroughly relieved.

2 tablespoons unsalted butter

2 tablespoons all-purpose flour

3 cups whole milk

2$\frac{1}{2}$ cups chicken stock

1 pound spinach, tough stems removed, thoroughly washed and patted dry

Fine sea salt and freshly ground black pepper

$\frac{1}{2}$ cup salt

$\frac{1}{4}$ cup tarragon vinegar

4 large eggs

In a medium pot, melt the butter over medium heat. Stir in the flour and cook, stirring, until you have a thick roux—that is, a thick smooth butter-and-flour mixture. Stir in the milk little by little, then the chicken stock. Add the spinach and bring to a boil, then reduce the heat and simmer for 5 minutes, or until the spinach is wilted.

Transfer the soup to a blender, in batches, and blend until smooth. Return the soup to the pot, season with salt and pepper, and keep warm over low heat.

Meanwhile, in a large pot, combine 4 quarts of water, the $\frac{1}{2}$ cup salt, and the tarragon vinegar and bring to a boil. Turn off the heat. Break 1 egg into a small bowl and gently lower it into the hot water with a large spoon. Repeat with the remaining 3 eggs. Poach for 5 to 8 minutes, depending on how cooked you like your eggs.

Pour the spinach soup into bowls. Add a poached egg to each and serve.

Porcini Consommé

SERVES 4

Adding a little cinnamon to the soup emphasizes the sweet spiciness of the mushrooms.

6 cups vegetable stock

1 pound porcini, cleaned, trimmed, and cut into ¹/₂-inch slices, or 1 pound button mushrooms, trimmed, cleaned, and sliced, plus 2 ounces dried porcini

5 black peppercorns

2 to 3 bay leaves

¹/₂ cinnamon stick

Fine sea salt

¹/₄ cup heavy (whipping) cream, whipped to soft peaks

¹/₂ teaspoon ground cinnamon

In a medium pot, bring the stock to a boil. Add the mushrooms, peppercorns, bay leaves, and cinnamon stick, reduce the heat, and simmer for 20 minutes. Skim off any foam that forms on the surface.

Line a colander or large metal sieve with cheesecloth and strain the consommé into another pot, pressing gently on the mushrooms with a spoon to release as much liquid as possible. Discard the mushrooms and spices.

Reheat the consommé and season with salt. Pour into bowls. Add a couple tablespoons of cream to each portion, sprinkle with cinnamon, and serve.

Frothy Cauliflower Soup with Chervil

SERVES 4 AS AN APPETIZER

AQUAVIT ADDS A NICE SPICINESS TO THE SOUP. IT'S AVAILABLE IN SOME LIQUOR STORES, BUT IF YOU CANNOT FIND IT, YOU COULD SUBSTITUTE MOCK AQUAVIT (PAGE 293). THE SOUP IS DELICIOUS WITHOUT IT, HOWEVER.

3 cups chicken stock

1/2 cup heavy (whipping) cream

1/4 cup dry white wine

1 firm large head cauliflower (about 1 1/2 pounds), core removed, cut into small florets

1 cup milk

4 tablespoons unsalted butter

1/4 cup aquavit (optional)

2 tablespoons finely chopped fresh chervil

In a medium pot, bring the chicken stock to a boil. Add the cream, white wine, and cauliflower; the cauliflower should be almost covered with liquid. Cook for 10 to 12 minutes, or until the cauliflower is soft.

Add the milk, butter, and aquavit, if using, and heat until simmering.

Transfer the soup to a blender, in batches if necessary, add the chervil, and blend until smooth and frothy. Pour into bowls and serve.

VARIATION: To give the soup more texture and substance, I like to add a few chunks of cooked diced chicken and reserved chunks of cauliflower just before serving.

Green Pea Soup with Garlic and Herbs

SERVES 4 AS AN APPETIZER

1 tablespoon unsalted butter

1 slice bacon, finely chopped

1 onion, chopped

2$\frac{1}{2}$ cups chicken stock

$\frac{1}{2}$ cup dry white wine

2$\frac{1}{2}$ cups shelled green peas

1 garlic clove, minced

1 tablespoon finely chopped
fresh dill

1 tablespoon finely chopped
fresh chervil

2 tablespoons heavy (whipping)
cream, whipped to soft peaks

Heat the butter in a deep sauté pan over medium heat. Fry the bacon for 3 to 4 minutes until crisp. Add the onion and cook, stirring, for 5 minutes, or until soft and lightly browned.

Add the chicken stock and white wine and bring to a boil. Add the peas and cook for 5 minutes, or until tender but still firm.

Transfer the soup to a blender or food processor and pulse until the peas are coarsely chopped. Add the garlic, dill, and chervil and puree until smooth.

Pour the soup into bowls. Add a tablespoon of whipped cream to each bowl and serve.

Traditional Yellow Pea Soup

SERVES 4

TRADITIONALLY THIS SOUP WAS MADE WITH A RICH STOCK FROM SMOKED PORK KNUCKLE. I USE A GOOD PORK OR BEEF STOCK AND SOME BACON.

10 ounces dried yellow peas, soaked overnight in cold water to cover, drained

1 tablespoon unsalted butter

2 slices bacon, finely chopped

1 onion, chopped

6 cups pork stock or beef stock

1/3 cup finely chopped celeriac

1/4 cup finely chopped leek, white and pale green parts only

1 small sprig fresh rosemary

1 bay leaf

1 tablespoon chopped fresh herbs, such as thyme, sage, and rosemary

Fine sea salt and freshly ground black pepper

Sour cream for serving

Heat the butter in a medium pot over medium heat. Fry the bacon for 4 to 5 minutes, until crispy. Add the onion and sauté for 5 minutes, or until soft and golden. Add the peas, stock, celeriac, leek, rosemary sprig, and bay leaf and bring to a boil, then reduce the heat and simmer gently for 1 hour, until the peas are starting to dissolve. Remove the rosemary sprig and bay leaf. Stir the soup energetically with a whisk or a wooden spoon until it has a somewhat smoother consistency.

Stir in the herbs. Season with salt and pepper to taste.

Pour the soup into bowls and serve with sour cream on the side.

Until recently, dried peas were an important part of the Norwegian diet, but they have now been almost entirely displaced by fresh or frozen peas. This is a pity, since the fresh and dried are not at all interchangeable.

While fresh peas are sweet and tender, dried peas are rich, rough, and starchy—on a cold winter day, nothing warms your body like a classic pea soup. (Note that the peas must be soaked overnight.)

Serve with bread and a small bowl of sour cream on the side.

2

THE BEST CURE

Gravlaks is a uniquely Scandinavian contribution to world cuisine, a way of preparing fish that is unlike anything else. While smoked salmon or dry-cured ham are variations on an almost universal theme, gravlaks is more difficult to categorize. The fish is not salty enough to be classified as salt-cured, nor is it cooked, but there is no mistaking it for raw fish dishes such as Japanese sushi or Mexican ceviche.

Today gravlaks is one of the most elegant and chic ways to serve up salmon. When someone puts a plate of thinly sliced gravlaks on the table, it is a sign of good taste, refinement, and appreciation of the guest. Yet, unlike many types of cured or smoked fish, it does not require much work or any special equipment to make it yourself.

Gravlaks has not always been such an easily enjoyable food. Originally, eating it was more of an extreme sport than a gastronomical pleasure. The word *gravlaks* means, literally, "buried salmon," and the first gravlaks was actually buried for the cure—wrapped in birchbark, placed in a hole in the ground, and covered with dirt. The salmon would spend several weeks or even months underground, and when unwrapped, it was almost inedible. But, as with cheese, the emphasis is on *almost*. The fermented fish made by the traditional gravlaks method can be compared to a mature raw milk cheese, with an odor that knocks you out. But, as with good cheese, its taste is milder. This hard-core version of gravlaks is today called *rakfisk* in Norway (where it can be made from a variety of fish) and *surströmming* in Sweden (made from herring), and it's not a delicacy for the fainthearted.

Today, making gravlaks no longer involves burial or a long fermentation period. It is a simple process of curing the fish in salt and sugar, often with dill and aquavit or brandy. Unlike the traditional method for *rakfisk,* it takes no more than four days. What makes it so special is that the curing process encourages autolysis, a process in which the cells and tissues of the flesh break up (technically, they are digesting themselves). The result is a softness similar to that of cooked or cured fish but with a freshness that sets it apart from all other treated fish products.

There is an intrinsic generosity to making gravlaks. In order to obtain the perfect result, you have to make at least two pounds or more of it, the ideal being to use two 3-pound fillets. That is more than a normal family of four would eat in a week or two, so in Scandinavia it is customary to invite guests to share it, or to give away some of it to friends and neighbors.

Making gravlaks is traditionally a household duty allocated to men. It is difficult to discover why this has been a masculine exercise, but one possible explanation springs to mind: It is a process so simple that even the most kitchen-phobic cook can do it.

Gravlaks with Sweet Mustard Sauce

SERVES 12 AS A MAIN COURSE, 20 AS AN APPETIZER

Two 3-pound salmon fillets, skin on, any pinbones removed

1/3 cup salt

2/3 cup sugar

1 tablespoon coarsely ground black pepper

3 tablespoons finely chopped fresh dill

1 teaspoon dill seeds

Sweet Mustard Sauce (recipe follows)

Rinse the fillets in cold water and pat them dry with paper towels. Combine the salt and sugar, and rub the flesh side of the fish with the mixture. Place one fillet skin side down in a deep dish just big enough to hold the fillets. Scatter the pepper, fresh dill, and dill seeds over it. Place the other fillet skin side up on top. Cover the dish with plastic wrap and place a heavy weight, such as two heavy dishes or a saucepan, on top of the fish. Refrigerate for 3 to 4 days, turning the fish every 12 hours and basting it with the brine that accumulates in the dish.

To serve, discard the brining liquid and brush off the dill. Slice the fish into thin slices on the diagonal with a sharp thin knife. The flesh from the tail will be leaner than the flesh from the belly. Serve with the mustard sauce.

Some cookbooks suggest freezing the salmon before you prepare it, to get rid of harmful microorganisms; with modern hygienic treatment of fish, this should not be a big issue. If you do freeze it, do it *after* it has been cured. Some of the proteins that may be damaged when freezing fresh fish will have broken down in the cured fish, so gravlaks can stand up to freezing better than fresh salmon can. The gravlaks will keep for up to 1 week in the refrigerator.

Gravlaks is normally served as one of many cold dishes in a buffet or smorgasbord, as we did on *New Scandinavian Cooking* in the Christmas program from Røros.

Serve with Sweet Mustard Sauce and scrambled eggs and dark rye bread for open-faced sandwiches, or with pickles and capers.

Sweet Mustard Sauce   MAKES 2 CUPS

6 tablespoons sweet grainy mustard, or to taste

2 to 3 tablespoons Dijon mustard

1 tablespoon sugar, or to taste

1 to 2 tablespoons vinegar

1 cup vegetable oil

2 to 3 tablespoons finely chopped fresh dill

Combine the sweet mustard and 2 tablespoons of the Dijon mustard in a medium bowl. Add the sugar and 1 tablespoon of the vinegar. Gradually add the oil, whisking constantly. Adjust the flavors as necessary. The sauce should be neither overly sweet nor overly acidic. Add a little water if the sauce gets too thick. Stir in the chopped dill. It will keep, refrigerated, for 2 to 3 weeks.

People tend to differ as to what the real, authentic food traditions are. These differences can cut across countries, regions, or even families (my wife and I can never agree on what to have for Christmas dinner). But on one subject, there is no disagreement among the people of Norway, Sweden, and Finland: Gravlaks should be served with a sweet mustard sauce.

Spicy Gravlaks with Aquavit

SERVES 6 TO 8

A FEW DROPS OF AQUAVIT, THE SCANDINAVIAN LIQUOR MADE FROM POTATOES AND FLAVORED WITH CARAWAY, LEMON PEEL, ANISEED, AND FENNEL, WILL GIVE GRAVLAKS A RICH, SPICY TASTE (SCOTCH OR AN EAU-DE-VIE ARE ACCEPTABLE SUBSTITUTES).

Two 1-pound salmon fillets, skin on, any pinbones removed

1 tablespoon caraway seeds

2 teaspoons aniseed

5 juniper berries

1/2 teaspoon crushed red pepper flakes or 1 small dried hot red chile pepper, seeded and chopped

1/2 teaspoon black peppercorns

3 tablespoons salt

1 1/2 tablespoons sugar

3 tablespoons finely chopped fresh dill

2 tablespoons aquavit, brandy, eau-de-vie, or Scotch

Rinse the fillets in cold water and pat them dry with paper towels. Crush the caraway seeds, aniseed, juniper berries, red pepper flakes, and black peppercorns using a mortar and pestle. Or place the spices on a cutting board or other hard surface and crush them with the underside of a heavy skillet. Combine with the salt, sugar, and dill.

Place one of the fillets skin side down in a deep dish just big enough to hold the fillets. Rub the fillet with half the spice and dill mixture. Rub the other fillet with the mixture and place it skin side up on top of the first. Pour the aquavit on top, cover the dish with plastic wrap, and place a heavy weight, such as two heavy plates or a saucepan, on top of the fish. Refrigerate for 3 to 4 days, turning the fish every 12 hours and basting it with the brine that accumulates in the dish. To serve, dust off some of the spices and slice the fish into thin slices with a sharp thin knife. The flesh from the tail will be leaner than the flesh from the belly. Serve with mustard sauce and dark rye bread, for open-faced sandwiches, or with mustard, pickles, and capers.

Juniper berries, fennel, allspice, and bay leaves are all traditional spices that offer a taste of the wild. On the more experimental side, a smoky barbecue sauce or smoked chipotle chiles will give the impression that the fish has been smoked as well.

Even if you do not cure your own gravlaks, the commercially cured fish you buy could benefit from a little bit of spicing up. You could simply pour a mixture of aquavit and crushed juniper berries over the fish, and give it an extra night in your own fridge before serving. The gravlaks will keep for 1 week.

Serve with Sweet Mustard Sauce (page 39) and New Potato Salad with Herbs and Green Beans (page 77) or Green Beans and Peas with Celeriac and Mango (page 230) and bread.

NOT GOOD ENOUGH FOR THE POOR, BUT A LUXURY FOR THE RICH

Today wild Atlantic salmon is considered one of the finest things you can eat, both expensive and hard to get. It has not always been like that. A few hundred years ago, salmon was the staple food of the poor and was held in low regard. In fact, lumbermen in Sweden and Norway often had clauses in their work contracts guaranteeing that they would not be served salmon more than five days a week. In Sweden's northernmost regions, money was scarce but salmon was plentiful, and as late as the seventeenth century taxes were still paid in the form of salmon.

For centuries, the salmon lived a double life. While in Scandinavia it was looked down upon as the simplest of all food, throughout the rest of Europe there was a salmon craze. British, French, and German aristocrats were willing to pay exorbitant sums for the fish that the bourgeoisie of the north would not touch. In France, smoked salmon from Sweden was twenty times more expensive than the finest cuts of veal or venison. And gradually Norway and Sweden became chic holiday spots for wildlife-hungry Europeans, an angler's paradise. Most Norwegians shook their heads in disbelief when they learned that British lords and Prussian businessmen were paying money to come to visit Norwegian rivers and fish their national fish.

Wilted Spinach with Smoked Salmon and Raspberries

SERVES 4 AS AN APPETIZER

½ cup crème fraîche or sour cream

16 raspberries

2 tablespoons Raspberry Vinegar (recipe follows) or white wine vinegar, or more to taste

1 to 2 teaspoons sugar

Fine sea salt and freshly ground black pepper

½ pound spinach leaves, tough stems removed, thoroughly washed and patted dry

Olive oil

8 to 12 thin slices smoked salmon

Pink peppercorns for garnish

Preheat the broiler.

To prepare the dressing, combine the crème fraîche, half the raspberries, the vinegar, and sugar in a small bowl. Season with salt and pepper. The dressing should be pleasantly tart.

Spread the spinach leaves on four ovenproof dinner plates. Sprinkle lightly with olive oil. Place the spinach under the broiler for 1 to 2 minutes, until the leaves have started to wilt. The spinach should not burn; however, don't worry if there are a few black patches on some of the spinach leaves—that just adds to the smoky flavor. Let the plates cool for 3 to 4 minutes.

Place the smoked salmon on top of the spinach, drizzle with stripes of the dressing, and garnish with the remaining 8 raspberries. Sprinkle with whole or crushed pink peppercorns.

Raspberry Vinegar

MAKES 2 CUPS

**20 raspberries, plus a few
for garnish (optional)**

2 cups white wine vinegar

Place the raspberries in a lidded jar or a bottle and pour in the vinegar. Let stand in a warm place, such as the window sill or next to the oven, for 2 to 3 days; shake the jar gently once a day.

Strain the vinegar and pour it back into the bottle. You might want to add a few fresh berries for decorative purposes, but they soon turn pale. It will keep, refrigerated, for up to 1 month.

The sweet tartness of raspberry vinegar makes it quite versatile, and it works well not only in dressings, but also in a wide variety of sweet and savory dishes. Sprinkle a few drops over fresh strawberries, or add a teaspoon or two to a hollandaise to go with fish. Although raspberry vinegar can be bought in most supermarkets, the best—and easiest—thing is to make your own.

Simple Salmon Mousse

SERVES 4 TO 6 AS AN HORS D'OEUVRE

This was the last dish we taped for
New Scandinavian Cooking, and it
was by far the simplest thing I made.
After almost a year of trying to prepare
food under extreme conditions,
it was a pleasure to finish off with
a dish as simple as this. There is
no cooking involved, just combining
the fish and crème fraîche in a
food processor.

½ **pound very fresh salmon fillet,
skin and any pinbones removed**

½ **pound smoked salmon,
skin removed**

3 **tablespoons fresh lemon juice**

**One 8-ounce container crème
fraîche or sour cream**

2 **tablespoons finely chopped
fresh dill**

2 **teaspoons pink peppercorns**

6 **tablespoons lightly salted shad
roe or lumpfish roe**

Toasts or crackers for serving

Rinse the fresh salmon under cold running water
and pat dry with paper towels. Remove any excess
traces of fat from the fillets. Cut both the fresh and
smoked fish into 1-inch cubes. Place the fish in a
food processor and process for a few seconds, until
you have a rough puree. Transfer to a bowl.

Stir the lemon juice, crème fraîche, and dill into the
salmon. Gently crush the pink peppercorns in your
hand and add them to the mousse. Gently stir the
roe into the mousse, being careful not to break the
fragile eggs.

Place a big dollop of mousse on top of each toast
or cracker, arrange on a platter, and serve.

Smoked Salmon, Asparagus, and Potato Cake Canapés

MAKES 32 TO 48 CANAPÉS

THE TRADITIONAL NORWEGIAN POTATO CAKE, THE *POTETLEFSE,* IS EXCELLENT FOR MAKING CANAPÉS OR FINGER FOOD.

¼ **lemon**

8 asparagus spears, trimmed

½ recipe Simple Salmon Mousse (page 46) or ½ pound thinly sliced smoked salmon plus ½ cup sour cream

8 potato cakes, blinis, or crêpes

6 tablespoons salmon roe

Small sprigs of fresh dill for garnish

To cook the asparagus, bring 4 cups salted water to a boil in a wide saucepan. Squeeze the lemon juice into the pot, then add the rind to the water (the lemon prevents the asparagus from discoloring during cooking). Add the asparagus and cook for 4 to 5 minutes, until tender but still firm in the center. Drain the asparagus and rinse under cold water to prevent further cooking.

Spread the salmon mousse on the potato cakes. (If you are using smoked salmon and sour cream, spread the sour cream on the potato cakes, then place the smoked salmon on top.) Place an asparagus spear on each cake and roll the cakes up around the asparagus. With a very sharp thin knife, cut each potato cake into 4 or 6 slices and arrange them on a serving plate cut side up. Add a little spoonful of salmon roe and a small sprig of dill to each canapé.

There is almost no limit to what you can match with a potato cake—in Norway, hot dogs are typically served wrapped in potato cakes instead of in rolls. For snacks, or with coffee, they may be served with sweet goat cheese, syrup, or honey.

Potato cakes can be bought in specialty shops or through the mail (see Mail-Order Sources, page 294).

L→R Simple Salmon Mousse, page 46. Smoked Salmon, Asparagus, and Potato Cake Canapés, page 47. Salmon Carpaccio with Lingonberries.

Salmon Carpaccio with Lingonberries

SERVES 4 AS AN APPETIZER

FOR THIS RECIPE, YOU WILL NEED SUSHI-QUALITY FISH. IF YOU ARE NOT SURE ABOUT THE FRESHNESS OF THE SALMON YOU FIND IN YOUR STORE, YOU CAN MAKE THIS DISH WITH SMOKED SALMON; IN THAT CASE, HALVE THE AMOUNT OF LIME JUICE.

LINGONBERRIES AND CRANBERRIES ARE CLOSE RELATIVES, AND CRANBERRIES CAN BE USED AS A SUBSTITUTE.

1 pound salmon fillet, skin and any pinbones removed, cut into thin slices, or 1 pound thinly sliced smoked salmon

2 tablespoons fresh lime juice (1 tablespoon if using smoked salmon)

2 teaspoons fleur de sel or 1 teaspoon regular salt

¼ cup lingonberries, halved, or cranberries, quartered

2 tablespoons finely chopped fresh parsley

2 teaspoons finely chopped red chile pepper (optional)

Arrange the salmon slices in one layer on four large serving plates. Brush with the lime juice. Let marinate for 15 minutes.

Sprinkle the salmon with the fleur de sel, lingonberries, parsley, and chile pepper, if using, and serve.

When I made this for *New Scandinavian Cooking,* we were in the middle of Namsen, one of Norway's best salmon rivers (and reportedly one of Franklin D. Roosevelt's favorite fishing places), so freshness was not an issue.

3

HOW WE SURVIVED: COD AND POTATOES

I am often asked how people can live in a place as cold as Norway. While I always feel slightly insulted by the question, it is indeed a very good one. How can people live in a country where the summer is no more than a short burst of ecstasy, a country of hills and mountains with less than 3 percent arable land, on the same latitude as Alaska?

The only answer I can think of is cod and potatoes—the gastronomical equivalent of luck and resilience.

The waters off the coast of western and northern Norway, where icy Arctic currents meet the warmer Gulf Stream, make an ideal breeding ground for cod. For centuries cod was one of the few commodities we had to offer the rest of the world. Cod, mackerel, herring, and animal hides were traded for wine, spices, books, and other luxuries that could make life in the high north more agreeable. This commerce linked Norway to the rest of Europe, culturally and economically, and gradually the modest trading posts along the coast grew into affluent cities like Bergen, Kristiansund, and Ålesund. Between the sixteenth and nineteenth centuries, more than 60 percent of all the fish consumed in Europe was cod, a good portion coming from Norway.

In fact, when Norway became an important seafaring nation, it was the search for cod that triggered the first journeys to the west, first to Iceland, then to Greenland. Leif Eriksson "the Lucky," the Norwegian-Icelandic Viking widely held to have been the first European to reach the shores of North America, was not looking for a continent to conquer. He had no great plans for building an empire. He was simply looking for new fishing grounds. He followed the cod from Iceland to Greenland, and farther still to North America (to what is now Labrador and Newfoundland). He named the new continent Vinland—"the Land

of Wine"—probably referring to the cranberries that the Vikings used to make wine, in their short but animated stay on the American continent. After a few years of a steadily deteriorating relationship with the local Indians, the Vikings gave up and returned home. But while southern Europeans were arguing about whether there was anything other

than an abyss on the other side of the Atlantic Ocean, Scandinavian maps showed the country named Vinland far off to the west.

More than five hundred years after Eriksson's "discovery," a native American crop arrived in Scandinavia. The potato found a hungry people, struggling to survive, and fewer than two hundred years after its arrival, it had become the staple food of the entire region. Potatoes would grow in poor soil and did

not seem to mind bad weather. They gave people one less thing to worry about, proving a much more nutritious, reliable, and high-yielding crop than grains and cereals.

Cod and potatoes are foods that encourage conservatism and experimentation, tradition and innovation. Both foods are nearly perfect as they are, and when they are served in all simplicity, few things can be better. Cod and potatoes can be subjected to infinite variations, served as a basic weekday supper or the pièce de résistance of a formal dinner.

Truffled Cod with Garlic-Veal Glace

SERVES 4

Four ½-pound cod fillets, skin on

1½ cups veal stock or 1 cup chicken stock plus ½ cup beef stock

8 garlic cloves

1 bay leaf

2 tablespoons all-purpose flour

Fine sea salt and freshly ground black pepper

4 tablespoons unsalted butter

1 tablespoon truffle oil

½ ounce fresh black truffle

Soak the fish in ice water for 15 to 20 minutes, or place it in a colander in the sink under cold running water for 15 to 20 minutes. Pat dry with paper towels.

In a small saucepan, bring the veal stock to a boil. Add the garlic and bay leaf and simmer gently until the garlic is soft and the veal stock is reduced to ⅓ cup, 15 to 20 minutes. Make sure the pot does not boil dry. Remove the garlic with a slotted spoon and set aside. Remove and discard the bay leaf.

Place the flour in a large dish and season with salt and pepper. Dredge the fish fillets in the flour. In a large nonstick skillet with a lid, heat 2 tablespoons of the butter over high heat. Add the fish, skin side up, and cook for 1 minute, then turn and cook for 2 to 3 minutes. Reduce the heat to medium, cover, and cook for 6 minutes, or until the fish flakes nicely with a fork. Remove from the heat.

Meanwhile, add the remaining 2 tablespoons butter and the truffle oil to the veal stock and heat over very low heat until the butter has melted; do not let boil. Add the reserved garlic.

Finely shave the truffle and scatter the shavings over the cod and into the cracks between the flakes of fish. Place the cod on warm plates. Drizzle with the garlic-veal glace and serve.

We featured this dish on the *New Scandinavian Cooking* show from Lofoten, an archipelago in northern Norway that is the center of the Norwegian cod fisheries.

I did the cooking in a beautiful old storehouse for dried cod, and although the recipe is pretty straightforward, it was not so easy to do. The temperature was less than 30 degrees and every time we stopped for close-ups, the food started to freeze. It took a while to prepare, but I have never eaten better cod than what we had during that intense week.

Serve with Wild Mushroom Ragout (page 221) and the Garlic Potato Purée from the recipe on page 48 or Potatoes with Goose Fat and Lemon (page 74).

Rosemary Cod with Vanilla-Scented Mashed Rutabaga

SERVES 4

Four ½-pound cod fillets, skin on

2 pounds rutabaga, peeled and cut into 1-inch dice

1 vanilla bean

8 tablespoons (1 stick) unsalted butter, cut into pieces

Fine sea salt

4 very small sprigs fresh rosemary

Freshly ground black pepper

1 tablespoon olive oil

Soak the fish in ice water for 15 to 20 minutes, or place it in a colander in the sink under cold running water for 15 to 20 minutes. Pat dry with paper towels.

Preheat the oven to 400°F.

Bring a large saucepan of lightly salted water to a boil. Add the rutabaga and cook for 25 to 30 minutes, until soft. Drain well.

Return the rutabaga to the pan to dry completely over low heat, 1 to 2 minutes. Puree the rutabaga in a food processor or pass it through a food mill, and return it to the pan. Cut the vanilla bean lengthwise in half. Scrape out the seeds and add to the mashed rutabaga. (Discard the bean or add it to a canister of sugar to make aromatic vanilla sugar.) Gently stir the butter into the mashed rutabaga until it melts. Season with a little salt. Keep warm.

Meanwhile, make a small incision through the skin of each cod fillet and gently insert a rosemary sprig. Season well with salt and pepper and rub with the olive oil. Place the fish in a roasting pan. Roast for about 15 minutes, until the fish flakes easily.

Place a large scoop of mashed rutabaga on each plate. Top with the fish and serve.

Scandinavians love the turniplike rutabaga (whose American name is derived from the Swedish word for rutabaga). One of the few vegetables to last through the winter, it was long the food of the poor, cherished as an important source of vitamins more than for its taste. When I was growing up, our old neighbor, the ascetic and ever-worried Mrs. Krigel, lived on rutabaga and boiled water for weeks at a time. "It is pure, good food," she insisted. "It will make you strong." Every time I visited her, she would insist that I eat a slice of raw rutabaga. She was sure that the sweet taste would take my mind off the chocolate and chewing gum she suspected me of devouring. Of course it didn't, and it was not until recently that I realized how wonderful this cheap, slightly sweet vegetable can be. Infused with the flavor of vanilla, it makes the most interesting contrast to lightly salted fresh cod.

The rutabaga can also be served with roast meats as an alternative to the somewhat plainer and more rustic Mashed Rutabaga (page 198).

Yellow and Red Cod with Pomegranate-Mango Salad

SERVES 4

This dish is a tropical explosion of colors and flavors. After all, cod was traded for—among other things—exotic spices, so why not combine them in homage to that heritage?

Serve with a green salad.

Four ¹/₂-pound cod steaks, skin on

1 tablespoon salt

2 teaspoons chili powder

2 stalks lemongrass, quartered lengthwise

1 teaspoon turmeric

A pinch of saffron threads or saffron powder

2 pomegranates

2 ripe mangoes, peeled, pitted, and cut into 1-inch chunks

2 tablespoons finely chopped shallots

1 tablespoon brandy or fresh lemon juice

1 tablespoon finely chopped fresh cilantro

Preheat the oven to 400°F.

Soak the fish in ice water for 15 to 20 minutes, or place it in a colander in the sink under cold running water for 15 to 20 minutes. Pat dry with paper towels. Rub with the salt and chili powder.

Crisscross the lemongrass stalks on a baking pan, making a rack for the fish. Place the fish on top of the lemongrass. Rub the right side of each steak with the turmeric and the left side with the saffron, so one half is bright yellow, the other orange-red. Roast for 10 to 12 minutes, until the flesh flakes easily.

Meanwhile, cut each pomegranate in half and remove the juicy seeds. In a large bowl, combine the pomegranate seeds, mangoes, shallots, brandy, and cilantro.

Divide the pomegranate-mango salad among four plates. Using a large spatula, place the fish on top, being careful to not let it fall apart (discard the lemongrass), and then serve.

Pan-Seared Cod with Garlic Potato Puree

SERVES 2

Serve as is or, for a taste of autumn, with some sautéed button mushrooms or Wild Mushroom Ragout (page 221).

Two ½-pound cod fillets, skin on

**4 cups chicken stock or
2 vegetable or chicken bouillon
cubes plus 4 cups water**

**1 pound russet potatoes, peeled
and cut into 1-inch dice**

4 large garlic cloves, peeled

**Fine sea salt and freshly ground
black pepper**

1 tablespoon olive oil

½ cup whole milk

**2 tablespoons heavy (whipping)
cream or half-and-half**

**4 tablespoons unsalted butter,
cut into small dice**

**1 tablespoon chopped fresh
parsley**

Soak the fish in ice water for 15 to 20 minutes, or place it in a colander in the sink under cold running water for 15 to 20 minutes. Pat dry with paper towels.

Meanwhile, make the potato puree: In a small saucepan, bring the chicken stock to a boil. Add the potatoes and garlic and boil for 10 to 15 minutes, until soft; drain. Return the potatoes and garlic to the pan and mash with a potato masher or pass them through a food mill or a potato ricer; return the mixture to the saucepan.

Season the cod fillets liberally with salt and pepper. Heat the oil in a large nonstick skillet over medium-high heat and add the fish, skin side up. Cook for 1 minute, then flip. Cook for 6 to 7 minutes more on medium heat, until the fish flakes willingly when pushed with a fork.

While the cod is cooking, combine the milk and cream in a small saucepan and bring to a simmer. Slowly stir the mixture into the potato puree, until smooth and velvety. Cook gently for 3 to 5 minutes, stirring constantly. Beat the butter and parsley into the potato puree. Season with salt and pepper to taste.

To serve, place the potato puree in the middle of two warm dinner plates, and set the cod on top.

L»R Pan-Seared Cod with Garlic Potato Puree. Cod Roe with Bay Leaf and Cucumber Salad, page 62.

COD ROE IS IN SEASON FROM LATE
FEBRUARY TO LATE MARCH. DURING THIS
TIME IT IS FOUND IN ABUNDANCE.
THE REST OF THE YEAR IT CAN BE HARD
TO FIND. YOU CAN REPLACE FRESH COD
ROE WITH LIGHTLY SMOKED COD ROE.
EVEN CANNED COD ROE IS THOROUGHLY
ENJOYABLE, BUT IF YOU SUBSTITUTE IT,
DO NOT COOK IT.

Cod Roe with Bay Leaf and Cucumber Salad

SERVES 4 AS AN APPETIZER OR 12 AS A CANAPÉ

Cod roe is one of the great under-estimated and underused ingredients. If Russian caviar is the foie gras of the sea, then cod roe is the equivalent of prosciutto—lean, elegant, and flavorful.

Because of its plenitude, cod roe has always been quite cheap, and this may be one reason why it has never gained the recognition it deserves. In Norway, it has always been considered delicious but never viewed as a delicacy. It is usually served simply as an integral part of the annual cod feast in late February that marks the beginning of the cod-fishing season in northern Norway.

1 fresh cod roe (about 1 pound)

1 cup salt

3 bay leaves, preferably fresh

1/2 lemon, cut into 8 thin wedges

1/4 cup vinegar

Freshly ground black pepper

1/4 cup sour cream

2 tablespoons chopped fresh chives

1/2 recipe Cucumber Salad (page 85)

Large round crackers if serving as a canapé (optional)

Gently clean the roe, removing all blood and tissue but making sure not to break the membrane. Place the cod roe on a sheet of parchment paper and season with about 2 teaspoons of the salt. Place the bay leaves and 2 lemon wedges on top. Fold the paper gently around the cod roe, as if you were wrapping a fragile present, and tie up the package with a piece of kitchen twine.

In a large pot, bring 4 quarts water to a boil. Add the remaining salt and the vinegar. Add the cod roe, reduce the heat, and simmer gently for 35 minutes. Lift the package out of the water and let cool.

Unwrap the cod roe. Remove and discard the bay leaves and lemon. With a sharp thin knife, cut the roe into thin slices. If you are serving this as an appetizer, transfer the roe to plates and season with pepper. Garnish with the sour cream, chives, and Cucumber Salad. If serving as canapés, place a slice of roe on each cracker, season with pepper, and top with the salad, sour cream, and chives. Arrange on a platter, garnish with remaining lemon slices, and serve.

Cod with Liver, Roe, and Sandefjord Butter Sauce

SERVES 4

LATE FEBRUARY AND EARLY MARCH IS THE SEASON FOR THE ANNUAL FAMILY COD DINNERS, A RITUAL WITHOUT WHICH MANY NORWEGIANS FEEL THAT SPRING WILL NEVER COME.

One 8-pound cod, gutted, cleaned, and cut into 1½-inch slices

½ pound fresh cod roe

½ pound fresh cod liver

½ cup red wine vinegar

2 bay leaves

1½ cups salt, plus more to taste

1 cup heavy (whipping) cream

8 tablespoons (1 stick) unsalted butter, cut into pieces

½ cup finely chopped fresh parsley

½ teaspoon finely grated lemon zest

2 teaspoons fresh lemon juice

Boiled new potatoes for serving

Lemon wedges for garnish

Soak the fish in ice water for 15 to 20 minutes, or place it in a colander in the sink under cold running water for 15 to 20 minutes. Pat dry with paper towels.

Carefully clean the roe and liver, removing all traces of blood. Bring 2 quarts water to a boil in a large saucepan. Add the vinegar, bay leaves, and ½ cup of the salt. Add the roe, reduce the heat, and simmer for 10 minutes. Add the liver and simmer for an additional 20 minutes.

Meanwhile, in a large pot, combine 4 quarts water and the remaining 1 cup salt and bring to a boil. Add the fish and return to a boil, then turn off the heat and let stand for 10 to 12 minutes, until the fish flakes nicely.

In a small saucepan, bring the cream to a boil. Add the butter, parsley, lemon zest, and lemon juice. Season with salt to taste. Keep warm over low heat.

With a slotted spoon, transfer the cooked liver, roe, and fish to a large serving platter. Serve with the butter sauce, potatoes, and lemon wedges on the side.

The traditional way to prepare cod is to cook it in salty water and serve it with its liver and roe and Sandefjord butter sauce, a cream-and-butter sauce with parsley. Because of its almost brutal simplicity, this dish demands a lot from your fish. Only a whole extremely fresh fish caught in very cold waters will do. I do not love cod liver, so I sometimes omit it. The fish is accompanied by simple boiled potatoes and, contrary to more continental traditions, served with red wine. Serving it with Cucumber Salad (page 85) would be a breach of tradition, but otherwise it is a fitting match.

The Sandefjord butter could also be served with salmon or halibut.

BACALAO: FAITHFUL STRANGER

As a Norwegian, I find that traveling or meeting people from faraway countries normally means having to explain what and where Norway is, sometimes taking great pains to pronounce the name slowly and clearly, so people are not led to believe that I am from "Nowhere." For some, the phonetic distinction between the two does not seem so important, but that is the price I have to pay for coming from a small, peaceful country tucked away far up north on the globe.

And yet there are times when I feel as though I come from a superpower, when people from far away surprise me with their immediate recognition and warm reception. "Ah, Norway/Noruega/Norvège," they say, always followed by the explanation for their enthusiasm: "Bacalao/bacalhau/baccalà/morue/ stockfish!" In Portugal, Spain, Brazil, Nigeria, Senegal, and parts of the Caribbean, Norwegian dried cod is considered one of the finest foods on earth.

Stockfish is cod that has been salted and dried, and therefore has a very long shelf life, much longer than the crudely dried unsalted cod. The particular method of salting and drying was introduced by the Dutch during the fifteenth century and was soon after adapted in Norway, Iceland, and Newfoundland. Dried cod had long been exported to parts of southern Europe, but as the Catholic Church started to enforce Lent and observe meatless days more vigorously, the demand for stockfish exploded. For centuries to come, dried salted cod was irreplaceable in most of the Catholic world. Between 1500 and 1800, 60 percent of all the fish consumed in Europe was cod, most of it dried, with a substantial share coming from Norway.

Contrary to what one might imagine, the dried fish is able to make sentiments run high. The Portuguese call the fish *fiel amigo,* "faithful friend," and quarrel loudly about which of their more than three hundred *bacalhau* recipes is the best. In Nigeria, the military government of General Sani Abacha faced broad social unrest when it introduced a luxury tax on Norwegian stockfish, making it virtually inaccessible for poor people and exorbitantly priced for the upper classes. And in Cuba, where

there is no longer the buying power for large-scale imports, I have friends who have traded a box of Cohiba cigars for a five-pound stockfish.

But as the Norwegian stockfish conquered the world, it remained a stranger in its own country, something to be relied upon as an important source of income but hardly ever eaten. It was not until the 1860s, when a boom in Norwegian-Spanish trade brought hordes of Spanish sailors and merchants to the western Norwegian towns of Kristiansund and Ålesund, the most important stockfish trading cities, that Norwegians first learned the true taste of bacalao, prepared with the most un-Norwegian of ingredients: tomatoes, pimientos, chiles, and olive oil. By the end of the century, when trade with Spain had diminished, the people of western Norway had adopted the bacalao as their own; some even eat it on Christmas Eve. In the rest of the country, however, bacalao has remained an oddity, something exotic eaten only by southern Europeans and the temperamental northwesterners from Ålesund and Kristiansund.

Bacalao Stew

SERVES 6

1½ pounds salt cod

2 pounds russet potatoes, cut into ½-inch slices

3 large yellow onions, cut into ½-inch slices

Two 14½-ounce cans tomatoes, chopped, with their juices

1 pound jarred or canned pimientos, drained and cut into ½-inch slices, or 1¾ pounds red bell peppers, roasted, peeled, seeded, and cut into ½-inch slices

4 to 6 garlic cloves, sliced

2 bay leaves

¼ cup chopped fresh parsley

1 to 2 dried hot red chiles, chopped and seeded

10 black peppercorns

1½ cups olive oil

Place the salt cod in a large pot of water and let soak for 24 to 36 hours, depending on how dry the fish is, until softened. Change the water at least twice during the process.

Drain the fish and cut into 2-inch chunks.

In a large pot, layer the potatoes, onions, and cod. Add the tomatoes, pimientos, garlic, bay leaves, two-thirds of the parsley, the chiles, peppercorns, and olive oil. Gently simmer for 30 minutes, then reduce the heat to low and cook for 45 minutes. Shake the pot every now and then, but do not stir.

Gently ladle the stew into six bowls, sprinkle with the remaining parsley, and serve.

You can make this dish a day in advance, and it tastes even better the second time around.

Serve with plenty of crusty bread.

Salt Cod with Peas, Mint, and Prosciutto

SERVES 2

Serve with potatoes or rice.

Two ½-pound lightly salted cod fillets, skin on (see Note)

1 tablespoon plus 2 teaspoons unsalted butter

1½ cups shelled green peas

2 tablespoons finely chopped shallots

2 tablespoons chopped fresh mint

¼ pound prosciutto, chopped

1 tablespoon lightly salted dried green snack peas or pistachios, crushed into a fine powder

Soak the fish in ice water for 15 to 20 minutes, or place it in a colander in the sink under cold running water for 15 to 20 minutes. Pat dry with paper towels.

In a large nonstick skillet, heat 1 tablespoon of the butter over medium-high heat. Add the fillets skin side down, and cook for 7 to 9 minutes, until the fish flakes easily with a fork.

Meanwhile, in a small pot, cook the peas in lightly salted boiling water for 3 to 4 minutes, or until tender but still firm. Drain the peas, return to the pot, and add the shallots, mint, prosciutto, and the remaining 2 teaspoons butter, tossing to mix. Reheat for 1 to 2 minutes.

Arrange the cod and peas on plates, sprinkle the cod with the dried peas, and serve.

NOTE: If you cannot find fresh salt cod, use fresh cod, soaked overnight in 4 cups water with 1 cup salt.

POTATOES: HUMBLE TUBERS

To my ninety-seven-year-old grandmother, nothing can be more perfect than a boiled potato. Whenever I make dinner for her, she is, despite her age, always curious to sample whatever new tastes I have brought home with me from my travels. She says it gives her a chance to partake in my journeys and sample the flavors of places she will never see. But, as is so often the case with traveling, the best thing is returning home. When she has finished her serving, she will compliment me, in her mild, generous manner, for showing her something new that she did not know existed. Then she will, with a smile, help herself to a boiled potato, peel it carefully but with surprising speed, and eat it with a big lump of butter. Seeing her contentment as she slowly eats the potato, I realize that no food can satisfy her more.

Potatoes have been a staple food in Norway for three centuries, and the cornerstone of almost every traditional Norwegian meal. Dinner would not be dinner without potatoes, and in an absurd attempt to make the new and exotic seem less intimidating, some of the first restaurants in Norway to serve spaghetti included a few boiled potatoes on the side.

Despite the introduction of pasta and rice, the potato still reigns. There are annual competitions to determine what varieties are best, from the small almond potatoes growing in the dry mountainous inland regions and the large, starchy Beate potatoes to the sweet, beautifully colored Golden Eye potatoes grown in northern Norway. Serving potatoes with almost every meal can be demanding for the cook, and although I by no means follow the rule that Norwegian food must be served with potatoes, I try to use the tradition as a challenge to discover the different qualities and the complexity of the humble tuber, from the luxury of a velvety smooth potato and garlic puree to the lightness of a new potato salad with chanterelles to the sweet comfort of caramelized potatoes.

A LUXURIOUS POTATO DISH, IF EVER
THERE WAS ONE. POTATO GRATIN
IS A GOOD SIDE WITH ALMOST ANY MEAT,
POULTRY, OR GAME DISH. RUTABAGA AND
PARSNIPS (OR POSSIBLY SOME SWEET
POTATO) ADD SWEETNESS AND FLAVOR.

Potato Gratin with Parsnips and Rutabaga

SERVES 6

2$^1\!/_2$ pounds russet potatoes, peeled and cut into $^1\!/_4$-inch slices

1 pound parsnips, peeled and cut into $^1\!/_4$-inch slices

1 pound rutabaga or sweet potato, peeled and cut into $^1\!/_4$-inch slices

2 bay leaves, preferably fresh, cut into 4 pieces

2 to 3 garlic cloves, cut lengthwise in half

2 cups whole milk

1 cup heavy (whipping) cream

$^1\!/_2$ teaspoon freshly grated nutmeg

1 teaspoon salt

Freshly ground black pepper

1 cup grated melting cheese, such as Gruyère

Preheat the oven to 300°F.

Put the potatoes, parsnips, and rutabaga in a baking dish and toss to mix. Insert the bay leaves and garlic throughout the vegetables.

In a small bowl, combine the milk and cream. Season with the nutmeg and salt and pepper to taste. Mix in half the cheese and pour the mixture over the potatoes.

Bake for 1 hour. Sprinkle with the rest of the cheese, turn the heat up to 350°F, and bake for 15 to 20 more minutes, until the cheese is nice and brown and the potatoes are tender.

Panfried Potatoes with Bay Leaves, Pancetta, and Mushrooms

SERVES 4 TO 6

THIS DISH GOES WELL WITH MOST MEATS.

4 slices pancetta or bacon, cut into ½-inch dice

2 teaspoons olive oil, if needed

6 large russet potatoes, cut lengthwise into 4 wedges each

1 to 2 bay leaves

Fine sea salt and freshly ground black pepper

2 tablespoons unsalted butter

½ pound portobello or button mushrooms, trimmed, cleaned, and cut into ¼-inch slices

2 teaspoons minced fresh thyme

Fry the pancetta in a large nonstick skillet until crisp. Remove it with a slotted spoon and set aside. If there is more than 1 tablespoon fat left in the pan, you will not need any olive oil; if not, add the oil. Add the potatoes to the pan. Crush the bay leaves in your hand and sprinkle them over the potatoes. Season with salt and pepper. Fry the potatoes over medium heat for 15 to 20 minutes, turning them from time to time to ensure that they cook evenly, until golden brown and tender.

Meanwhile, melt the butter in a large skillet over medium heat. Sauté the mushrooms for 3 to 4 minutes, or until tender. Season with salt and pepper and the thyme.

In a large bowl, toss the mushrooms, potatoes, and pancetta to mix. Serve.

VARIATION: I like the way the potatoes taste when they are pan-roasted, but if you want, you can bake them instead. Place the potatoes in a roasting pan or large baking dish, toss with the fat, and season them as above. Bake at 400°F for 30 minutes, or until golden brown and tender.

Serve with Oven-Dried Tomatoes (page 240) and Yogurt-Mint Sauce (page 265).

GOOSE AND DUCK FAT ARE THE MOST
FLAVORFUL FATS THERE ARE, AND WHEN
THEY ARE USED FOR COOKING POTATOES,
THE HUMBLE TUBERS BECOME WONDER-
FULLY FLAVORFUL AND AROMATIC.

Potatoes with Goose Fat and Lemon

SERVES 4

6 russet potatoes, peeled and
cut into wedges

Fine sea salt and freshly ground
black pepper

3 tablespoons goose or duck fat

½ lemon, cut into wedges
or strips

3 bay leaves, broken in half

Preheat the oven to 400°F.

Season the potato slices generously with salt and pepper.

In a large frying pan, heat the goose fat until hot. Add half the potato slices and cook, turning once, for 6 minutes, or until they have a crisp surface. Transfer to a large baking dish. Repeat with the remaining potatoes. Place the lemon wedges and bay leaves in between the potatoes.

Bake for 25 to 30 minutes, until the potatoes are tender. Discard the lemon wedges and bay leaves before serving.

Caramelized Potatoes

SERVES 4 TO 6

If possible, try to find potatoes that are no bigger than walnuts. I wash the potatoes thoroughly but normally peel them only if the skin is very rough.

2 tablespoons unsalted butter

¼ cup sugar

2 pounds very small new potatoes, cooked in boiling salted water until tender, drained, and peeled, if desired

½ teaspoon salt

1 teaspoon chopped fresh lemon thyme or other thyme

In a large nonstick skillet, melt the butter over low to medium-low heat. Stir in the sugar and cook until melted and light brown, stirring constantly with a wooden spoon to make sure the sugar does not burn. Add only as many potatoes as will fit without crowding the pan, season with salt and thyme, and cook, shaking the pan constantly to make sure the potatoes are coated on all sides, until slightly browned and caramelized. (You can gently push the potatoes around in the pan, but make sure not to break them.) Transfer the potatoes to a serving platter and cover to keep warm. Repeat with the remaining potatoes and serve immediately.

VARIATION: When I serve these potatoes with game, I add 2 crushed juniper berries to the caramel, and when I serve them with lamb, I sprinkle the potatoes with a little finely chopped fresh dill just before serving. Adding a little bit of chopped garlic can be good when serving them with beef or chicken.

New Potato Salad with Herbs and Green Beans

SERVES 4

THIS IS A LOVELY POTATO SALAD THAT IS BEST MADE FROM THE SWEET FIRST NEW POTATOES OF SUMMER. IT MAKES GREAT PICNIC FOOD, SINCE IT CAN BE MADE A FEW HOURS, OR EVEN A DAY, IN ADVANCE.

$2\frac{1}{2}$ pounds small new potatoes

Fine sea salt

$\frac{2}{3}$ pound green beans

A large handful of chopped mixed fresh herbs, such as mint, thyme, parsley, and/or basil

2 garlic cloves, crushed

2 tablespoons capers, drained

1 tablespoon grated lemon zest

$\frac{1}{2}$ cup extra virgin olive oil

3 to 4 tablespoons fresh lemon juice

Freshly ground pepper

Edible flowers (optional)

Place the potatoes in a saucepan and add 1 tablespoon salt and enough water to cover generously. Bring to a boil and cook for approximately 15 minutes, until the potatoes are tender but still firm in the center (use a fork to check whether the potatoes are done). Drain the potatoes and allow to cool slightly, then cut them in half and place them in a large bowl.

Meanwhile, cook the beans in lightly salted boiling water for 4 to 5 minutes, until just tender. Drain. Add the beans to the warm potatoes, then add the herbs, garlic, capers, and lemon zest. Combine the oil and lemon juice in a measuring cup, pour over the potato salad, and toss to mix well. Season with salt and pepper. Let stand for a few hours at room temperature so that the herbs will have time to flavor the potatoes. Sprinkle with edible flowers, if desired, just before serving.

New Potatoes with Chanterelles and Dill

SERVES 4

THIS DISH IS ONE OF MY LATE-SUMMER FAVORITES. IT CAN BE SERVED HOT, WARM, OR COLD. THE POTATOES GO WELL WITH RICH, FATTY FISH LIKE MACKEREL OR SALMON, AND WITH GAME, LAMB, AND BEEF.

2 pounds small new potatoes

2 tablespoons unsalted butter

½ pound chanterelles, trimmed, cleaned, and halved (quartered if large)

Fine sea salt and freshly ground black pepper

1 to 2 garlic cloves, finely chopped

2 tablespoons finely chopped fresh dill

1 tablespoon finely chopped fresh parsley

Place the potatoes in a large pot and cover with lightly salted water. Bring to a boil for 15 to 20 minutes, or until tender; drain and let cool slightly.

Meanwhile, in a large skillet, heat the butter over medium-high heat until it bubbles enthusiastically. Add the chanterelles and cook for 4 to 5 minutes until tender. Season with salt and pepper. Add the garlic and cook for 1 more minute. Remove from the heat.

Cut the potatoes in half and put them in a bowl or a deep serving plate. Add the mushrooms and toss to mix well. Sprinkle with the dill and parsley and toss well again before serving.

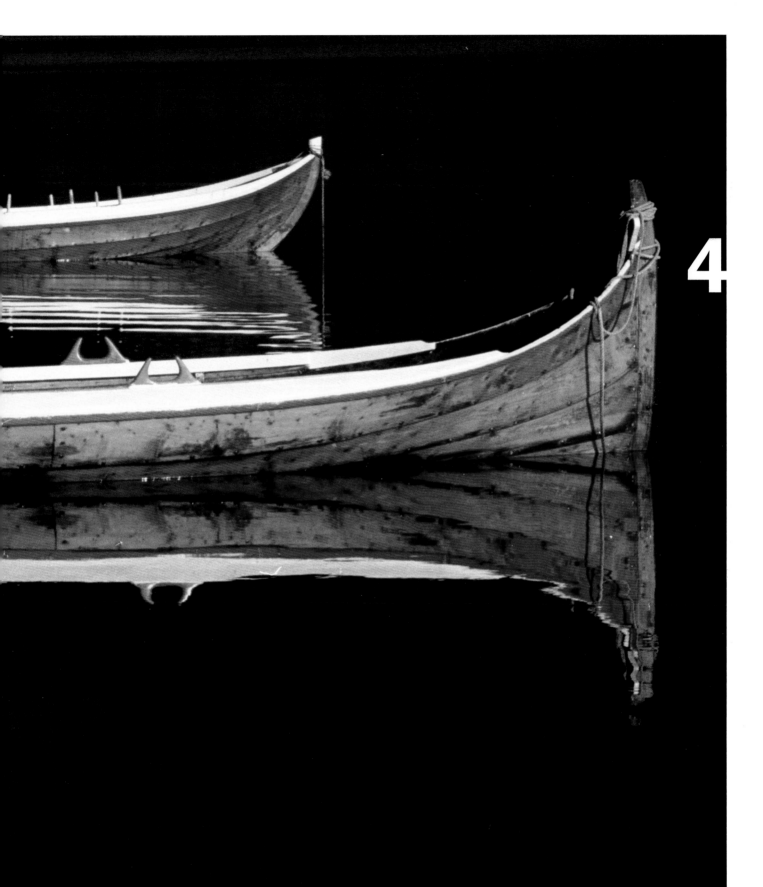

4

A MIDSUMMER NIGHT'S FEAST

The morning air is thick with anticipation, and the grass is still cold with dew when we head down to the boathouse. Only three grown-ups and two children can fit in the old flat-bottomed rowboat. The boat smells of tar and salt, and the oars bite into my hands as I row slowly out toward our net. Once we have reached the bright yellow buoy marking the beginning of the big net, the kids hang over the boat's gunwale, scouting for the shimmering silver of the salmon in the dark water. "I can see something down there! I can see something down there!" they whisper excitedly, most of the time just seeing their own reflections in the waves. Then we start pulling our way through the net. It is heavy and cold, and sometimes a sea nettle has been caught in it, making your hands even sorer. Everyone is quiet, sensing the authority of this ancient tradition—you don't play around or make noise in a small rowboat when you are out inspecting the salmon nets. And then we see the big strong body of a silvery fish coming toward

the surface, still struggling in the net. Once the fish is brought on board and untangled, and the rest of the net examined, we turn back toward the boathouse and breakfast. By the time we arrive, the boat is covered in shimmering silver dust from the scales of the fish. "We always get a good catch when you come along," I hear my father-in-law whisper to his daughter, as he always does when they go fishing together. And, as always, I can see it makes my wife proud, giving her the extra strength to carry the big, heavy fish up to Grandma's house.

On good days, there can be as many as ten salmon caught, causing the net to get all tangled up around the powerful fish. Sometimes it takes hours just to get the net untangled without damaging the fish.

Even during summer, the water is cold—it seldom reaches 60 degrees before July—and

the strong ocean wind makes the sun feel more like a giant light-bulb than a provider of heat. When we are finished, it takes enormous amounts of hot coffee to warm us up again. But the fish is more than worth the effort.

There are few things more beautiful than the Atlantic salmon. Just before it heads toward the rivers, the fish is at its best. The flesh is wonderfully pink and tasty after two or three years of feasting. As an extra bonus, the abdomen of the females is full of beautiful orange roe—like a hidden treasure of soft, shiny pearls.

By midsummer, our freezer is full of salmon. Most of it we send off to Uncle Ole, who salts and

smokes the fish to perfection over juniper and oak wood shavings in his own smokehouse.

The finest specimen is reserved for the great midsummer night's feast. On the longest day of the year, when it never really gets dark, all the men are sent off, and all the women prepare the traditional salmon dinner. The salmon is cooked early in the day, and placed on the landing to cool (with a heavy weight placed on the lid to prevent cats from helping themselves). As the guests start arriving in the evening, it is customary to show them the fish, encouraging them to comment on it and to share their best fishing stories.

If the weather is fine, we eat on the lawn outside the red house. The table is decorated with daisies and lilacs. The long summer night, with its famous Nordic light, veils everything in its pastel hues. The shiny pink flesh of the fish, gently cooked, skinned, and served cold; the fresh light green cucumber salad; the bright yellow new potatoes, no bigger than eggs and wonderfully sweet; the green dill; and the white sour cream—the pastel beauty of it all is like a romantic midsummer night's dream. A master chef could not create anything more beautiful. At the beginning of the meal, I always think we have far too much food, that a twenty-pound fish is too much for twenty-five people, including some normally fish-phobic children. But no matter how big the fish is, we always manage to finish it off, with a bit of help from the cat.

Poached Salmon with Horseradish Sour Cream

SERVES 8

THIS IS THE CENTERPIECE OF THE TRADITIONAL MIDSUMMER NIGHT'S FEAST. THE FISH IS FLAVORED WITH BAY LEAVES, BLACK PEPPERCORNS, AND CORIANDER AND SERVED COLD. WHEN IT IS ALLOWED TO COOL IN THE COOKING WATER, THE FISH DEVELOPS A DEEP, ALMOST SHELLFISHLIKE FLAVOR.

One 16-ounce container sour cream

2 teaspoons grated horseradish

2 to 3 tablespoons fresh lemon juice

1/2 cup salt

1/4 cup white vinegar

20 black peppercorns

2 bay leaves

1 tablespoon coriander seeds

2 to 4 whole cloves

2 teaspoons dried thyme

One 7-pound salmon, cleaned and scaled

1 recipe Cucumber Salad (recipe follows)

Boiled new potatoes for serving

To prepare the horseradish sour cream, combine the sour cream and horseradish in a bowl. Add lemon juice to taste. Cover and refrigerate.

To prepare the fish, bring 1½ gallons water to a boil in a pot large enough to hold the fish. Add the salt, vinegar, peppercorns, bay leaves, coriander, cloves, and thyme. Place the fish in the pot, return the water to a boil, and turn off the heat. When the water has cooled to lukewarm, remove the fish. Serve, or cover and refrigerate for up to a day before serving.

Serve with the horseradish sour cream, Cucumber Salad, and boiled potatoes.

VARIATION: If you do not have a pot big enough for the fish, you can cut it into 3 pieces. The fish will not look as impressive, but the taste will be the same. You can also season the fish with 3 tablespoons salt, the bay leaves, pepper, and coriander, wrap it in foil, and bake it at 350°F for 1½ hours.

Cucumber Salad

SERVES 8 AS A SIDE DISH

1 tablespoon coarse sea salt

3 to 4 cucumbers, peeled and thinly sliced

1/2 cup white wine vinegar

2 teaspoons sugar

1/2 teaspoon freshly ground white pepper

1/3 cup water

Sprinkle half the salt in the bottom of a large deep dish or bowl. Place the cucumber slices in the dish. Sprinkle with the rest of the salt. Place another dish or bowl on top of the cucumbers, hold them tightly together, and shake well to extract some water.

Combine the vinegar, sugar, and white pepper in a bowl. Add 1/3 cup water. Pour the mixture over the cucumbers and let stand for an hour before serving.

Honey-and-Mustard-Marinated Salmon with Rosemary Apples

SERVES 2

Serve with sour cream and New
Potatoes with Chanterelles and
Dill (page 79).

**1 pound salmon fillet, skin on,
any pinbones removed**

2 tablespoons olive oil

1 tablespoon honey

2 tablespoons Dijon mustard

1 garlic clove, minced

1 tablespoon fresh lemon juice

1 teaspoon chili powder (optional)

Fleur de sel

**4 sweet apples, such as
Golden Delicious**

2 tablespoons unsalted butter

1 small sprig fresh rosemary

**Fresh mint leaves for garnish
(optional)**

Rinse the fish under cold running water. Pat dry
with paper towels.

In a shallow dish, mix the olive oil, honey, mustard,
garlic, lemon juice, and chili powder, if using. Place
the fish in the mixture, turning to coat it with the
marinade. Cover and marinate for 2 to 3 hours in the
refrigerator or, if pressed for time, for 30 minutes
at room temperature.

Preheat the oven to 375°F.

Transfer the fish to a baking dish. Bake for about
12 minutes, or until the flesh flakes nicely with a
fork. Season with salt.

Meanwhile, core the apples and cut each into
8 wedges. Heat the butter in a large skillet over
medium-high heat. Add the apples and rosemary,
reduce the heat to medium, and cook for 5 minutes,
until tender. Remove from the heat and discard
the rosemary.

Serve the fish with the apples, garnished with mint,
if desired.

VARIATION: Reserve the marinade. After 8 minutes
of baking, pour the marinade over the salmon. Serve
the salmon with the pan juices spooned over it.

WILD OR FARMED?

The wild Atlantic salmon is a unique and vulnerable fish. It lives most of its life in the ocean but can spawn only in freshwater. Every one of these fish has a special homing device that scientists have yet to account for, and after roaming around in the Atlantic Ocean for two or three years, covering tens of thousands of miles, the fish returns to the same riverbank, only a few feet from where it was hatched, to spawn.

For every five thousand salmon eggs that are laid on sandy riverbanks, only five fish live to reach the ocean. Of these five, only one survives long enough to return home and spawn again. This is a cycle that is vulnerable to overfishing and the effects of human enterprise.

With increased industrialization and fishing, wild Atlantic salmon has become an exclusive food, reserved for the rich and powerful—or for those, like my wife's family, who are lucky enough to have fishing rights where the last remaining wild salmon meet. Luckily, modern aquaculture has given the salmon back to the people. Today the quality of farmed fish is generally very high, although it is often somewhat fattier than wild salmon.

If you have the choice between wild and farmed salmon, you should naturally opt for the wild one—at least if it is very fresh and the price is just slightly higher than the farmed fish. But when the price is double or triple, you will be paying more for the romantic idea of the fish fighting its way up the rivers than for actual flavor.

THE SPICES USED IN THIS RECIPE—DILL SEEDS, CUMIN, CORIANDER, FENNEL, AND CARAWAY—MAKE THE DISH SEEM DISTINCTLY MIDDLE EASTERN. BUT THE SAME SPICES ARE ALSO IMPORTANT IN SCANDINAVIAN COOKING—IN FLAVORING AQUAVIT, THE TRADITIONAL SPICED POTATO LIQUOR—SO YOU WILL FIND THE SAME WHIFF OF SPICES IN ALMOST EVERY SCANDINAVIAN HOME AROUND CHRISTMASTIME.

Spice-Crusted Salmon with Aquavit Sour Cream

SERVES 2

I made this dish on the *New Scandinavian Cooking* program when we filmed on the River Namsen. I prepared the salmon fillet with the skin left on because it is less likely to fall apart during cooking.

Serve with Baked Fennel (page 236) or boiled potatoes.

1 pound salmon fillet, skin on, any pinbones removed

2 teaspoons coriander seeds, crushed

2 teaspoons cumin seeds

2 teaspoons dill seeds

2 teaspoons fennel seeds

1 teaspoon salt

¼ cup fresh lemon juice

¼ cup sour cream

1 tablespoon aquavit or Mock Aquavit (page 293) (see Note)

1 teaspoon caraway seeds

1 tablespoon finely chopped fresh chervil

2 teaspoons white wine vinegar, or to taste

1 recipe Baked Fennel (page 236)

Rinse the fish under cold running water. Pat dry with paper towels.

In a small skillet, toast the coriander, cumin, dill, and fennel seeds over medium heat for about 2 minutes, until they start to release their fragrance. Transfer to a small bowl, add the salt, and mix well.

Rub the fish with the spice mixture and place in a baking dish. Sprinkle with 1 tablespoon of the lemon juice. Cover and let marinate in the refrigerator for 1 to 2 hours.

To prepare the aquavit sour cream, in a small bowl, mix together the sour cream, aquavit, caraway seeds, and chervil. Add vinegar to taste. Cover and refrigerate.

Preheat the oven to 350°F.

Place the baking dish with the fish on the middle oven rack and bake for 12 to 15 minutes, until the fish flakes nicely with a fork.

Serve the fish topped with the sour cream and accompanied by the fennel.

NOTE: If you cannot find aquavit, season the sour cream with ¼ teaspoon ground fennel seeds, ¼ teaspoon ground dill seeds, ¼ teaspoon ground cumin seeds, 1 teaspoon sugar, and 1 tablespoon brandy.

Slow-Baked Salmon with Soy Sauce and Ginger

SERVES 2

COOKING FISH AT VERY LOW TEMPERA-TURES MAKES IT JUICIER AND MORE TENDER THAN THE TRADITIONAL HIGHER HEAT. EXACTLY HOW LONG THE COOKING TAKES DEPENDS ON YOUR OVEN. THIS COOKING PROCESS DEMANDS THAT YOU USE VERY FRESH FISH. IF YOU WANT TO PREPARE THIS DISH USING THE MORE CONVENTIONAL HIGH-TEMPERATURE COOKING PROCESS, FOLLOW THE BAKING INSTRUCTIONS GIVEN FOR SPICE-CRUSTED SALMON (PAGE 90).

1 pound salmon fillet, scaled, skin on, any pinbones removed

¼ cup soy sauce

3 tablespoons finely chopped ginger

Preheat the oven to 140°F.

Rinse the fish under cold running water. Pat dry with paper towels.

In a small saucepan, bring the soy sauce to a boil and boil for 3 minutes, or until reduced by one-third. Remove from the heat.

Place the salmon in a baking dish. Brush the salmon with the soy sauce. Sprinkle with half the ginger.

Bake about 45 minutes, until the temperature in the center reaches 120°F on an instant-read thermometer. Sprinkle with the remaining ginger and serve.

Both soy sauce and fresh ginger have become popular over the last few years as a consequence of recent Asian influences on Scandinavian cooking, but they are in no way novelties. Ginger has been known in Norway since the fourteenth century, soy sauce since at least the early nineteenth century. Both work very well with salmon.

Serve with Green Beans and Peas with Celeriac and Mango (page 230) and Cumin-Baked Parsnips with Salmon Roe (page 241; feel free to omit the salmon roe and sour cream).

Salt-Baked Salmon with Simple Chervil Mayonnaise

SERVES 4

This recipe is adapted from Eyvind Hellstrøm, the chef-owner of Restaurant Bagatelle in Oslo, a luxurious, modern restaurant with two stars in the Michelin *Guide Rouge*. The salt-baking technique is very simple and can be used with other fish as well, even with lean fish like cod.
The idea is to season the fish from the top and cook it from the bottom, and the result is a deliciously salty, wonderfully tender fish.

Baked Fennel (page 236) and a salad make perfect accompaniments.

Four ½-pound salmon fillets, scaled, skin on, any pinbones removed

About ¼ cup fleur de sel

2 large egg yolks

Juice of 1 lemon

½ cup olive oil

½ teaspoon cayenne pepper

2 teaspoons finely chopped fresh chervil

Scrape the salmon skin with a knife to make sure all the scales are removed. Rinse well and pat the fish dry with paper towels.

Heat a large nonstick or cast-iron skillet over medium-high heat (no oil is needed). Place the fillets skin side down in the pan, without crowding. Cover the flesh side of the fish with the salt and cook for about 10 to 12 minutes, until the fish is nearly done. (If the fish is very fresh, I like it best when rare. If you are not so sure about the freshness of the fish, give it an extra minute or two.) Transfer to a plate.

While the fish is cooking, whisk together the egg yolks and one-third of the lemon juice in a small bowl. Whisk in a drop of olive oil; when the oil is completely incorporated, whisk in another drop. Continue adding the oil little by little, whisking continuously, then add more lemon juice until you have a fresh-tasting mayonnaise. (You may not need all the lemon juice.) Whisk in the cayenne pepper and chervil until well blended.

Gently brush the salt from the fish. Place one salmon fillet on each serving plate, and place a dollop of mayonnaise on top of each. Serve the remaining mayonnaise on the side.

5

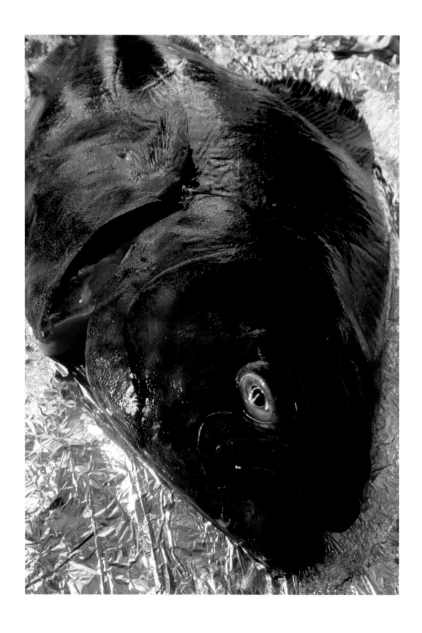

TALKING FISH

I once kissed a fish.

It was in no way a romantic "I love you" kiss, nor a passionate "I want you" kiss, rather a quick, cautious kiss of the kind that is normally reserved for old aunts and remote French acquaintances. But these clarifications do not really make a difference, for it was a kiss. For a split second, my lips were in contact with the cold, wet skin of the fish—before I hastily retreated.

When I was a child, I loved the fairy tale of the fisherman who caught a talking flounder. As a trade-off for its release, he got three wishes. (As is so often the case with slightly moralizing fairy tales, he got greedy and ended up back where he started.) So when a shouting halibut landed in my boat, I was perplexed. It did not behave as fish should behave, for fish— I have always been told—are not supposed to make any sound. The shouts were low and hoarse, as if from a human trapped in a cave, and for a few seconds its eyes looked almost human. I held the hammer in my hands but

I could not simply end its life without knowing for sure that it was not in fact something more than a fish. As my more cynical fishing companions were busy pulling in the rest of the net, I tried talking to the fish. There was no reply. That is when I did it: I gave it a quick kiss. The fish responded with another shout, sounding genuinely appalled, then it started flapping violently. When nothing else happened—it did not transform into a beautiful princess, nor did the shouting turn comprehensible—I whacked it on its head and returned to cleaning out the net.

I have always felt somewhat shameful of my, if not directly indecent then at least not quite seemly, conduct that day nearly fifteen years ago. It was only just lately that I found out that I am in good company, and that my behavior is at least in accordance with centuries of folk mythology. Almost all cultures have seen something magical in the halibut.

From the American Indians of the Pacific Northwest to the nomadic peoples living in northern Norway thousands of years ago, the halibut has been regarded as a god-fish. It is even evident in the name: Halibut is derived from *Holy but,* "the holy flatfish."

On the bare rock surface outside Alta in northern Norway, archaeologists have found six-thousand-year-old rock carvings showing fishermen pulling large halibut into small canoes. Next to the carvings of halibut, there are images with strongly erotic subjects, almost pornographic. It is not possible to know exactly what link these early Norsemen, of whom we know very little, made between the halibut and sexuality, but it is evident that hoisting a large halibut into a small canoe was seen as a feat of manhood.

Even today fishermen in northern Norway will tell you that in order to catch a halibut, you need to have a certain sexual aura, known as *hall.* *Hall* is something a fisherman can obtain by having intercourse with a woman the night before he goes fishing. "If it is a good woman, and the sex is satisfying to them both," one fisherman told me bluntly, "then he will catch a big halibut the next day." It is the story of aphrodisiac food turned on its head: While prosperous societies where food is plentiful create confidence-building myths about food's ability to improve their sex lives, the ancient people of northern Norway, living at subsistence level near the margins of what is humanly possible, saw food as much more important than sex. They created another kind of confidence-building myth, one where the aim was to muster the courage to face the dangers of the sea, and in that way secure survival.

You do not have to be a believer in ancient mythology to see what is special about the halibut. Even the dry facts about the fish are enough to intrigue: A halibut, which can weigh as much as six hundred pounds, starts its life swimming upright like most other fishes, with one eye on each side of its head. When it has put childhood behind it, it lies down on one side, in the halibut's case, the left side. Slowly but determinedly, the left eye moves over to the right side of the face. The upper side of the fish turns black, and the underside retains its shiny white skin. And as if that were not enough, the halibut has a peculiar air bladder, and when the fish is kept out of water, it sometimes gives off hoarse, insistent shouting sounds—which should not be mistaken for a cry for help or a longing for lip contact.

Herbed Halibut with Rosemary-Lemon Butter

SERVES 4

When I made this dish on *New Scandinavian Cooking,* I baked a twenty-pound halibut in the sand, using the same cooking technique used by our ancestors many centuries ago and by New Englanders for their clambakes. While I've adapted the recipe for a home kitchen, the ingredients are the same, and the results very similar. Use a good wine, one you enjoy drinking yourself.

Serve with New Potato Salad with Herbs and Green Beans (page 77) or Onion Pie with Jarlsberg and Thyme (page 223).

Four ¹/₃-pound halibut steaks

Fine sea salt

1 cup plus 2 teaspoons chopped fresh parsley

1 cup chopped mixed fresh herbs, such as thyme, tarragon, mint, sweet balm, and/or rosemary

5 bay leaves, preferably fresh, finely chopped

2 teaspoons dried or fresh marigold (optional)

2 garlic cloves, chopped

¹/₂ cup dry white wine

8 tablespoons (1 stick) unsalted butter

1 tablespoon finely chopped fresh rosemary

1 teaspoon finely chopped fresh thyme

1 teaspoon finely chopped fresh tarragon

1 teaspoon finely grated lemon zest

2 to 3 tablespoons fresh lemon juice

Freshly ground black pepper

4 pesticide-free marigolds for garnish (optional)

Rinse the fish under cold running water and pat dry with paper towels.

Rub the halibut steaks on both sides with 2 teaspoons sea salt. Combine the 1 cup parsley, the chopped mixed herbs, four-fifths of the bay leaves, the marigolds, if using, and the garlic and rub onto both sides of the fish. Place the fish in a deep baking dish, cover, and refrigerate for at least 30 minutes, or up to 24 hours.

Preheat the oven to 400°F.

Pour the wine over the fish and cover the baking dish with foil. Bake for 15 to 20 minutes, until the fish is opaque throughout and comes away from the bone when tested with a knife.

Transfer the halibut to a platter and cover to keep warm. Pour the pan juices into a small saucepan and reduce over medium heat to about ¹/₄ cup.

Meanwhile, in another small saucepan, heat 1 tablespoon of the butter until it bubbles enthusiastically. Add the finely chopped rosemary, thyme, and the remaining bay leaves. Cook for 2 minutes. Add the rest of the butter and let it melt, then add the tarragon, the remaining 2 teaspoons parsley, and the lemon zest. Simmer for 3 to 4 minutes; do not boil. Add the lemon juice, the reduced marinade, and salt and pepper to taste. Strain the sauce and discard the herbs.

Brush off the herbs from the fish. Place a halibut steak on each plate, and place a marigold, if using, on the side. Pour a little rosemary-lemon butter over each halibut steak and serve.

VARIATION: When increasing the quantity of fish, you do not need to increase the amount of wine and herbs accordingly. Use enough herbs to cover the fish and enough wine to cover the bottom of the pan. Bake until the fish is opaque throughout and comes away from the bone when tested with a knife. If you are cooking a large halibut, you should use an instant-read thermometer; the fish is done when the interior temperature has reached 125°F.

THE FINE, FIRM FLESH OF HALIBUT HAS
A WONDERFUL, ALMOST SHELLFISHLIKE
SWEETNESS TO IT, A QUALITY THAT IS
EMPHASIZED BY PAIRING THE FISH WITH
VANILLA. THIS IS JUST AS GOOD SERVED
COLD. IF YOU CANNOT FIND GOOD
HALIBUT, USE SEA BASS INSTEAD.

IF THE HOLLANDAISE SAUCE BREAKS,
ADD 1 TABLESPOON COLD WATER OR AN
ICE CUBE AND WHISK ENERGETICALLY
UNTIL SMOOTH AGAIN.

Vanilla-Scented Halibut with Asparagus and Hollandaise

SERVES 4

One 1½-pound halibut steak

Fine sea salt

½ vanilla bean, split lengthwise in half

½ cup dry white wine

8 tablespoons (1 stick) unsalted butter

2 large egg yolks

2 tablespoons fresh lemon juice

2 pounds white or green asparagus, trimmed

Freshly ground black pepper

Preheat the oven to 400°F.

Rinse the fish under cold running water and pat dry with paper towels.

Place the fish in a small baking dish and rub with sea salt. Scrape out the small black seeds from the vanilla bean with the back of a knife and rub them over the fish. Cut the scraped bean into small pieces and place them on top of and underneath the fish. Pour over the white wine, cover tightly with aluminum foil, and bake for 20 to 30 minutes, until the fish is opaque throughout and the interior temperature reaches about 125°F on an instant-read thermometer.

Meanwhile, melt the butter in a small saucepan over medium-low heat. In a small bowl, whisk together the egg yolks and lemon juice. Whisk in the melted butter and return the mixture to the pan, whisking constantly over low heat until thickens. Remove the sauce from the heat and whisk for 2 minutes. Set aside in a warm spot.

Cook the asparagus in a large pot of generously salted water until tender but still firm, 5 to 8 minutes. Drain, season with pepper, and cover to keep warm.

When the halibut is done, transfer it to a platter and cover to keep warm. Pour the pan juices into a small saucepan and reduce to ¼ cup.

Cut the halibut into 4 pieces and place on plates. Pour the marinade over the fish, add the asparagus, top with a little hollandaise, and serve.

BUYING FISH

Whether I am in Norway or in the States, I always try to make time to buy my fish at a proper fish market. The best way to ensure that the fish you buy is fresh is by looking and touching—fresh fish should smell pleasantly salty and sweet, not fishy; the eyes should be clear; and the gills should have a healthy red or pink color and not be slimy. However, since inspecting the fish up close is not often encouraged, the second best is to ask questions: Where is the fish from? When was it caught? Has it been frozen? If the person selling the fish cannot answer these questions, the likelihood is that you would not have liked the answers anyway, and if you buy the fish, you should make sure to clean it properly and cook it until well done, not rare.

If a recipe calls for raw or only semi-cooked fish, ask your fishmonger for sushi-quality fish.

If you do not have a good fish market where you live, the best alternative is often to buy frozen fish (see Mail-Order Sources, page 294). High-quality frozen fish can be very good, but it needs to be defrosted very slowly in the refrigerator. Slow thawing can take up to twenty-four hours, but it is more gentle to the flesh.

You may from time to time find that your fish market has a variety of fish but not the specific fish mentioned in your recipe—in which case it will usually be fine to substitute another, related fish.

White lean fish can usually be replaced by other white lean fish, and fatty fish with other fatty fish. The result will not always be the same as intended, but better than if you used the fish called for but of inferior quality.

Here are a few fish that are interchangeable in most recipes:

Haddock and turbot.

Cod, pollock, haddock, and scrod.

Salmon, rainbow trout, and Arctic char.

Mackerel does not have any close relatives that can easily be used as replacements, but recipes calling for mackerel are normally good made with other small fatty fish, such as river trout.

MACKEREL AND CHANTERELLES ARE TWO OF THE BEST THINGS OF LATE SUMMER, AND THE TWO GO VERY WELL TOGETHER. SEASONING FATTY FISH WITH CURRY POWDER IS QUITE COMMON IN NORWAY, AND EVEN MY CONSERVATIVE GRANDMOTHER, NOT NORMALLY A SPICE ENTHUSIAST, USES IT WHEN FRYING TROUT OR MACKEREL.

Crispy Mackerel with Chanterelles

SERVES 4

Serve with Cucumber Salad (page 85), Potatoes with Goose Fat and Lemon (page 74), and sour cream.

Four 1-pound mackerel, cleaned

Fine sea salt

1/2 lemon, cut into thin slices

1/4 cup chopped fresh chives

1/4 cup all-purpose flour

1/2 teaspoon curry powder

Freshly ground black pepper

6 tablespoons unsalted butter

1 pound chanterelles, trimmed and cleaned, or 1 pound button mushrooms, trimmed and cleaned, plus 1 ounce wild mushrooms

2 garlic cloves, crushed

2 teaspoons fresh thyme leaves

1 tablespoon red wine vinegar

Rub the mackerel with 1 tablespoon salt. Fill the cavities with the lemon and two-thirds of the chives. In a large bowl, combine the flour and curry powder; season with salt and pepper. Dredge the mackerel in the flour mixture so they are lightly coated.

In a large cast-iron or other heavy skillet, heat 2 tablespoons of the butter over medium-high heat until melted and light brown. Add the fish and cook, turning once, for 6 to 7 minutes. Reduce the heat to medium-low and continue cooking for approximately 8 minutes, or until the fish is cooked through. To test for doneness, insert a metal skewer into the flesh; if it comes out warm, the fish is done.

While the fish is cooking, heat the remaining 4 tablespoons butter in a separate large skillet over medium heat. Add the chanterelles, garlic, and thyme and cook for 2 to 3 minutes. Add the red wine vinegar, reduce the heat to medium-low, and cook for 4 to 5 more minutes. Add salt and pepper to taste. Remove from the heat. Just before serving, add the remaining chives to the mushrooms.

Place 1 mackerel on each plate, put the chanterelles next to the fish, and serve.

Grilled Mackerel with Sweet Chili Glaze and Charred Sage

SERVES 4

MACKEREL IS QUITE FATTY, SO IT IS PERFECT FOR GRILLING. IT LOOKS GOOD, SO I ALWAYS SERVE THE FISH WHOLE. HOWEVER, ITS SKIN TEARS EASILY, SO YOU NEED SOMETHING TO PROTECT IT. I COVER IT WITH SAGE LEAVES, WHICH GIVE THE FISH A NICE SMOKY HERBAL FLAVOR AS THEY ARE CHARRED.

Four 1-pound mackerel, cleaned

1 tablespoon fine sea salt

1/2 lemon, cut into 4 wedges

1/4 cup chopped mixed fresh herbs, such as oregano, dill, and rosemary

1/2 cup packed brown sugar

1 tablespoon chili powder, or more to taste

2 tablespoons water

1 tablespoon soy sauce

A small handful of fresh sage leaves

Heat a gas grill to medium-high, or prepare a hot fire in a charcoal grill.

Rub the mackerel with the salt. Fill the cavity with the lemon wedges and chopped herbs. Cut 3 or 4 small slits into each side of the fish.

In a small nonstick saucepan, combine the sugar, chili powder, water, and soy sauce and bring to a boil over medium heat. Add more chili powder if needed. Brush the mackerel with the hot glaze and cover with the sage leaves.

Place the fish on the grill and grill for 8 to 10 minutes on each side. To test for doneness, insert a metal skewer into the flesh; if it comes out warm, the fish is done.

Place a fish on each plate and serve. I leave the sage leaves on for the guests to remove, as the fish will start to fall apart when you remove the sage.

Serve with Broccoli with Capers, Garlic, and Anchovies (page 231), Oven-Dried Tomatoes (page 240), and Yogurt-Mint Sauce (page 165).

Monkfish with Bacon, Mint, and Wild Mushrooms

SERVES 4

Monkfish is undoubtedly the ugliest fish in the sea, and in Norway it was until recently considered inedible— I know people who, in the 1960s, were ahead of their time and were able to get free monkfish every day.

Neither fishermen nor most customers had the courage to deal with a monster like the monkfish, so they never found out that beneath the frightening, slimy gray surface there is a wonderful and tasty white flesh. Nowadays, however, monkfish is held in high regard, and it is one of the most expensive fish in the market.

Serve with New Potato Salad with Herbs and Green Beans (page 77) or Potatoes with Goose Fat and Lemon (page 74), and Yogurt-Mint Sauce (page 165).

One 2-pound skinless monkfish fillet

1 cup chopped fresh mint

4 slices bacon or prosciutto

1 tablespoon vegetable oil

1 tablespoon sugar

1 tablespoon olive oil

1 to 2 tablespoons fresh lemon juice

3 tablespoons unsalted butter

1 pound wild mushrooms, such as chanterelles or porcini, trimmed, cleaned, and cut into 1-inch pieces

Fine sea salt and freshly ground black pepper

Preheat the oven to 350°F.

Rinse the fish under cold water and pat dry with paper towels. Rub the fish on both sides with one-third of the mint. Wrap the bacon around the fish and secure with toothpicks.

Heat the vegetable oil in a large nonstick skillet over medium-high heat. Sear the fish, turning twice, for 5 to 6 minutes, until the bacon is turning crisp and brown and has rendered some of its fat.

Transfer the fish to a baking dish, reserving the fat in the skillet. Bake the fish for 15 to 20 minutes until opaque.

Meanwhile, using a mortar and pestle, crush the remaining mint with the sugar and olive oil until you have a smooth mixture (or use a food mill or food processor). Season with the lemon juice.

Heat the butter with the reserved bacon fat in a large skillet over high heat until it bubbles enthusiastically. Add the mushrooms and cook for 2 to 3 minutes, then reduce the heat to medium and cook for 4 to 5 minutes. Season liberally with salt and pepper.

Cut the fillet into 4 pieces and serve with the mushrooms and mint sauce.

6

IN THE LAND OF THE MIDNIGHT SUN

It is 3 A.M. and the sun is still shining brightly as our boat gently puffs out from Harstad harbor toward the open sea. I am tired from only an hour and a half of sleep, but the skipper, Geir, a teacher in his late fifties, says that soon the light will tell my body that it is daytime, and the fatigue will go away.

"When you have gone a few days without sleep, then you start feeling really tired," he says. "You Southerners always have a bit of a problem adapting." Norwegians like me, who live south of the Arctic Circle, are always referred to as Southerners. Even if our winter is cold and long too, it is just not the real thing. "We who live here have figured it out. We stay awake during summer and sleep through the winter."

Harstad is two hundred miles north of the Arctic Circle. Here, in the Land of the Midnight Sun, the year has a different rhythm from the rest of the world. During the winter months, the sun never rises above the horizon—only a few hours of dusk around noon remind you that the sun will come back, that you are not experiencing an eternal night, although it may feel that way. But summer makes up for all the darkness. From June to August, the sun never sets. Late at night it heads down toward the horizon and just nearly makes it before changing its mind and rising again. During the summer holidays, children visit each other at 2 A.M., and friends go swimming in broad daylight at midnight. And I am in a small fishing boat at 3 A.M., heading out to the rich fishing banks right off the coast.

Geir lights up his pipe and opens a beer. It is still a few hours until he has to go to work, so he can treat himself to a Mack beer, a slightly bitter pilsner brewed in the northernmost brewery in the world—and the traditional accompaniment to the northern Norwegian specialty *måsegg,* cooked seagull eggs stolen from the nests just after they are laid.

The sea is dark blue and calm, and there is hardly a ripple on the surface. "Look over there," Geir says, and points toward the big open sea. "The sea is boiling." As we approach, I see what he is talking about. There seems to be a furious fight in the water; thousands of fish are fighting ferociously, or perhaps conducting a wild and beautiful underwater ballet. Suddenly they disappear, and a few seconds later they surface a hundred feet from the boat. Sometimes they split into two groups, and once they surround the boat and I can see them up close, shining silver, gray, and blue.

Slowly Geir takes out the line. He knows that if he rushes, the hooks will only be tangled up. With calm, confident movements, he releases the line into the water. Ten seconds later, he starts pulling it in. On each of the six hooks there is a pollock. They make

rapid swimming movements, trying to get away, and then suddenly seem to move willingly toward us. Two of them fall off as they are hoisted into the air, but Geir knows that there will be more. We continue to follow the fish around, and after less than five minutes, we have more than fifty fish in our enormous bucket.

"That will be enough for all my kids and their families. If this isn't richness, then I don't know what is."

We anchor in a small lagoon to make breakfast. The water is almost turquoise, and so clear that you can see crabs, small fish, and sea anemones thirty feet below. Geir boils some seawater while I rinse the fish. I can still feel them moving in my hands when I put them into the boiling water. We eat the fish in complete silence, with only parsley, bread, and margarine. I drink Mack beer and Geir drinks coffee. I had no idea that something so simple— and eaten with margarine—could be so good. You always eat more

boiled fish than you do fried or seared, especially when served with such simplicity. Still, I am surprised to realize that we must have eaten more than a pound each.

"Well, just about now the sun is rising in Paris and Rome," Geir says when we have finished. "They probably have no idea what they have been missing." He makes a gesture toward the blue sea and the sun—high up in the sky by now.

"But enough, it's about time we head back." Geir has to be at work in an hour and a half.

Poached Pollock with Parsley Butter

SERVES 4

THIS IS PROBABLY THE EASIEST WAY TO SERVE POLLOCK, AND IF YOU HAVE VERY FRESH FISH, IT IS ONE OF THE BEST, PRESERVING ALL THE FLAVORS OF THIS UNDERRATED AND GENERALLY INEXPENSIVE FISH. IF YOU CANNOT FIND FRESH POLLOCK, USE WHITE LEAN FISH, SUCH AS COD AND SAITHE. IF YOU CUT DOWN A LITTLE ON THE PARSLEY BUTTER, THIS BECOMES A LEAN, HEALTHY DISH.

4 small pollock or 3 pounds pollock fillets, cut into 2-inch pieces

1/2 cup salt

3 tablespoons white wine vinegar

2 bay leaves

12 black peppercorns

8 tablespoons (1 stick) unsalted butter, diced

2 tablespoons finely chopped fresh parsley

1 garlic clove, crushed

1 anchovy fillet

1/2 teaspoon finely grated lemon zest

1 tablespoon lemon juice

Fine sea salt and freshly ground black pepper

Soak the fish in ice water for 15 to 20 minutes, or place it in a colander in the sink under cold running water for 15 to 20 minutes. Pat dry with paper towels.

Combine 4 quarts water and the salt in a large pot and bring to a boil over high heat. Add the vinegar, bay leaves, and peppercorns, drop the fish into the boiling water, and return to a boil. Turn off the heat and let the fish cook in the hot liquid for 7 to 9 minutes.

Meanwhile, to prepare the parsley butter, combine one-third of the butter, the parsley, garlic, anchovy, lemon zest, and lemon juice in a small saucepan; heat over medium heat until the butter melts. Cook for 2 minutes to release the flavors, then reduce the heat to medium-low and gradually whisk in the rest of the butter. Season with salt and pepper and remove from the heat.

Drain the pollock and place on individual plates. Drizzle each serving with some of the parsley butter and serve immediately, with the remaining butter on the side.

Serve with boiled potatoes or bread and some mustard. I alternate between Dijon mustard and sweet grainy mustard.

Parsley-Steamed Pollock with Chile, Mussels, and Clams

SERVES 2

THIS IS ONE OF MY FAVORITE WAYS TO SERVE POLLOCK, SLIGHTLY SPICY AND WITH A NICE HERBAL SWEETNESS FROM THE PARSLEY. I NORMALLY PLACE THE SKILLET DIRECTLY ON THE TABLE—THAT WAY, THOSE I AM COOKING FOR CAN SEE THE FISH BEFORE IT FALLS APART, AS IT INEVITABLY DOES WHEN YOU MANEUVER IT ONTO YOUR PLATES.

1 pound pollock fillet,
skin removed

1 tablespoon olive oil

1 small onion, finely chopped

1 small red chile, seeded and
finely chopped

1 garlic clove, finely chopped

1 bunch fresh parsley, stems
removed and reserved, leaves
chopped

Fine sea salt

10 mussels, scrubbed under cold
running water and debearded

10 whole small clams, scrubbed
under cold running water

1/2 cup dry white wine

1 tablespoon unsalted butter,
diced

Soak the fish in ice water for 15 to 20 minutes, or place it in a colander in the sink under cold running water for 15 to 20 minutes. Pat dry with paper towels.

Heat the olive oil in a skillet with a tight-fitting lid over medium-high heat. Add the onion, chile, and garlic and cook for about 5 minutes, until the onion is soft and lightly browned. Add the parsley stems to the skillet, making a bed for the fish. Season the pollock fillets with salt and place them on top of the parsley stems. Arrange the shellfish around the fish, pour the wine over the fish, and put the lid on. Let the fish and shellfish steam over medium heat for 7 to 9 minutes.

Add the chopped parsley and the butter to the pan and wait just until the butter has melted into the cooking juices, then serve immediately. Transfer the fish and shellfish to shallow soup plates, discard the parsley stems, and pour the cooking juices around the fish. Serve with bread to sop up the broth.

POLLOCK: A RETURN TO THE TABLE

"Did you catch anything?"

"Nah, just a few pollock."

For anyone who has been fishing off the coast of Norway, Denmark, or Sweden—or off the East Coast of the United States—these words may sound oddly familiar. Whenever you throw out a line—no matter how lousy a fisherman you are, how rusty your hook is, or how empty the ocean may seem—there is always a pollock down there, just waiting to be caught. In Norway, where fish is abundant, it has almost always been greeted with the same lack of enthusiasm. "I was expecting a nice big cod or dreaming of a beautiful wild salmon, or an equally ugly monkfish, and this is what I got. Mr. Common Fish."

In fact, the pollock seems more eager to get caught than fishermen are to catch it. Sound like an exaggeration? I don't think so—because once I caught the same fish twice in a row. I was out fishing for cod and had almost secured a lovely dinner for the entire family when the pollack bit the first time. It was a sad-looking, shiny fish with big, watery eyes that made it look apologetic

rather than edible. I uttered the standard words: "Nah, just a pollock." The hook was in the left side of its mouth, and it wasn't difficult to get out. Since I was fishing for cod, I released it back into the water. But in less than two minutes, it was back in the boat. This time the hook was on the right side, and the small wound from the recent encounter with the hook was still visible on the left. It was as if it was begging me: "Take me with you. Let me become soup, feed me to your cat. Just get me out of this cold, dark place."

Because of its abundance, pollock has never really been appreciated. Like so much food eaten by the poor, those who could afford to opt for more exclusive fish did so, presuming that you get what you pay for. The pollock wasn't rediscovered in Norway until 1998. The young and talented Norwegian chef Terje Ness went to Lyon, France, to participate in the prestigious Bocuse d'Or—the unofficial world championship of cooking. He made a stunning creation using Norwegian pollock and scallops, with which he captured the hearts and

The pollock revival took two equally interesting directions. It gave us license to experiment with new flavor combinations. Inspired by Terje's success in Lyon, artistic combinations of pollock—with Italian truffles, or Thai chiles, or Spanish chorizo—started appearing on restaurant menus all over Scandinavia, giving the pollock a sleek, modern image. But, more important perhaps, it also gave Norwegians a revived pride in our traditional recipes. The old working-class preparation of Seibiff *med løk* (seared pollock fillets with caramelized onions) was suddenly back on dinner tables, even among urban professionals, and—slightly revamped—in trendy bistros.

And now, if you ask someone who has been out fishing whether they caught anything, you should not be surprised if they answer, "*Ja.* Yes, I certainly did. I caught the most beautiful pollock."

Pollock has more taste than most fish, but it is still relatively cheap. When it is poached, steamed, or gently seared, you can truly taste the fine flavors of the North Sea.

palates of the judges. Terje was awarded the world championship—snatching it from under the noses of shocked Frenchmen—and the pollock was invited back to kitchens and tables throughout Scandinavia and beyond.

THIS IS RUSTIC FOOD, AS SIMPLE AND
TASTY AS YOU COULD DESIRE. WHEN
ONIONS ARE COOKED FOR A LONG TIME,
THEY BECOME WONDERFULLY SWEET
AND AROMATIC. THE ONIONS CAN BE MADE
UP TO ONE DAY IN ADVANCE.

Seared Pollock Fillet with Caramelized Onions

SERVES 4

Serve with boiled potatoes and a mixed green salad.

2 tablespoons unsalted butter

6 large yellow onions, cut into 1/3-inch slices

2 teaspoons sugar

2 whole cloves

One 1 1/2-pound pollock fillet, skin on, cut into 4 equal pieces

Fine sea salt

2 teaspoons all-purpose flour

2 to 3 tablespoons bacon fat or butter

Freshly ground black pepper

Heat the butter in a large skillet over medium heat. Add the onions and cook for 10 minutes, tossing the onions around every once in a while. Add the sugar and cloves and cook for 15 more minutes over medium-low heat, stirring occasionally, until the onions are soft, brown, and sweet. Keep warm over low heat.

Meanwhile, soak the fish in ice water for 15 to 20 minutes, or place it in a colander in the sink under cold running water for 15 to 20 minutes. Pat the fish dry with paper towels.

Rub the fillets with salt and dredge them in the flour. Heat the bacon fat in a large nonstick skillet. Add the fish skin side up and cook for 1 minute, then turn and cook for 5 to 7 minutes more, until flaky.

Remove the cloves from the onions and discard. Distribute the onions among four plates, place the fish on top, season with pepper, and serve.

7

OUT ON A LIMB

It is the small thrills that give life its spice, not the big, well-planned adventures. One of the small things that makes my lazy summer days something more than just idle recreation is harvesting mussels from the bare rock face just a few feet from the boathouse of our southern Norwegian summer house. It is the perfect thing to do on days when the sun is shining from long before you awake till almost midnight, when even going out on the fjord to catch a few fish seems like too much of an effort. There are not many days like that in Norway, so every minute of them is savored, knowing that it might well be another year until the next time cold wind, clouds, and rain agree to leave us alone.

It is nearly dinnertime before I manage to break free from my idleness. I head down to the sea, still wearing shorts and sandals. In my right hand I carry a rake; in the left, a bucket. Carefully I climb out on the steep rocks, getting as far out as possible without stepping on the wet stones by the waterline. I use the rake to remove a few dozen mussels from the rocks immediately below the surface of the sea. There are many more farther down, in a small crack in the rock, but they are just out of reach from where I am standing.

This is the point when my heart starts beating harder. Very gently I place one foot on the wet, slippery stone surface, trying to find the perfect balance between reaching farther into the colony of mussels and not falling into the water. From my new position, I manage to reach a whole lot of mussels, but they are clinging more tightly to the surface than the others, so I have to pull the rake toward me with a powerful jerk. This time my left foot slips, and I almost fall. My foot finds support at the last moment, and I am saved from the disgrace of splashing violently into the water—although I am not sure how much grace I am really left with. From a distance, my

struggle for balance must look like slapstick shadowboxing, a clumsy fight against an unseen adversary.

I am almost doing a split and I am as wobbly as ever, but my bucket is nearly half full. Just a few more mussels, and no one will have to leave the dinner table hungry. From where I am standing, all the best-looking shells, those that are neither too old nor too small, are within my reach. In less than five minutes, my bucket is full. I even throw out a few mussels I do not like the looks of, those that are overgrown with algae or seaweed and are a pain to wash.

It is now that I realize I cannot move. There is no way I can move my left foot out of the water without falling, jeopardizing my entire catch. I contemplate my options for a few seconds, but I see none.

From the house, I can hear someone shouting. I said I would be only ten minutes. People are probably getting hungry. Someone will be on the way soon, and I would rather not be seen in this helpless position—doing a split, unable to move. I make a quick decision. I throw the rake and bucket ashore and submerge myself in the cold, clear water. The water is certainly refreshing, not as unpleasantly cold as I had feared.

I look like a drowned cat, and my wet sandals are making loud squeaking noises as I approach the house. The mussels hardly need washing, and twenty minutes later they are on the table, steamed with garlic and thyme and served with only stewed mushrooms, bread, butter, and lots of white wine. We eat greedily, but when we are finished, there still seems to be a mountain of mussels left in the huge pot.

"Did you fall into the sea?" someone wonders. A newcomer.

"Of course not. I jumped," I reply, trying to sound offended.

"It doesn't make sense, though," one of my regular summer guests says. "First you try your best to rake in the mussels while balancing on the slippery rocks. And when you are done, you jump willingly into the water. Why do you always do that?"

I have no answer except, perhaps, that that's the way my best summer days are supposed to be.

Mussels with Aquavit, Cream, and Tarragon

SERVES 2 AS A MAIN COURSE, 4 TO 6 AS AN APPETIZER

THIS IS A RICH, FILLING WAY OF SERVING MUSSELS. MAKE SURE TO HAVE A LOT OF GOOD BREAD TO SOP UP ALL THE JUICES.

2 pounds mussels, scrubbed under cold running water and debearded

1 tablespoon unsalted butter

3 tablespoons finely chopped shallots

1 garlic clove, crushed, plus 1 more to taste

1 tablespoon chopped fresh tarragon

1 teaspoon chopped fresh thyme

2 teaspoons tarragon vinegar

1 teaspoon fennel seeds

1 tablespoon aquavit or brandy

2 tablespoons heavy (whipping) cream or crème fraîche

Fine sea salt

Throw out any mussels with cracked shells or that did not close when you scrubbed them.

Heat the butter over medium heat in a pot just large enough to hold the mussels. Sauté the shallots and garlic for 4 to 5 minutes. Add half the tarragon, the thyme, vinegar, fennel seeds, aquavit, and mussels. Increase the heat to medium-high. Cover and let steam for 6 to 7 minutes, until the mussels have opened. With a slotted spoon, transfer the mussels to a large serving bowl; discard any that did not open.

Add the cream to the cooking juices and cook over medium-high heat for 3 minutes, until slightly reduced. Season with salt and a little more minced garlic, if desired. Pour the cooking juices over the mussels, sprinkle with the rest of the tarragon, and serve.

Thyme-and-Garlic-Steamed Mussels with a Hint of Cinnamon

SERVES 2 AS A MAIN COURSE, 4 TO 6 AS AN APPETIZER

If you are in search of a less subtle dish, the mussels have enough strength and individuality to stand up to powerful spices like chiles or piri-piri. How tasty the dish ends up, though, is to a large extent dependent on how good a white wine you use. If it isn't a wine you enjoy drinking, you will probably not like it with the mussels either.

A whiff of cinnamon blends in nicely with the mussels, enhancing their sweetness.

Serve with bread and butter, or mayonnaise flavored with a little saffron.

2 pounds mussels, scrubbed under cold running water and debearded

2 tablespoons olive oil

2 to 3 garlic cloves, chopped if you want a milder taste, crushed if you want a stronger one

1/6 cinnamon stick

2 to 3 sprigs fresh thyme

1 cup good dry white wine

2 tablespoons unsalted butter

2 tablespoons finely chopped fresh parsley

2 teaspoons finely grated orange zest

Throw out any mussels with cracked shells or that did not close when you scrubbed them.

Heat the oil in a pot just large enough to hold the mussels. Sauté the garlic for 2 to 3 minutes. Add the cinnamon stick, thyme, mussels, and wine. Cover and let steam for 7 to 8 minutes, until all, or nearly all, the shells have opened. Transfer the mussels to a serving bowl; discard any that have not opened.

Bring the cooking juices to a boil and cook for 4 to 5 minutes to concentrate the broth and to extract more taste from the thyme and cinnamon. Strain the liquid and discard the solids. Return the liquid to the pot. Stir in the butter and pour over the mussels. Sprinkle with the parsley and orange zest and serve.

Mussel Fricassee with Wild Mushrooms and Arugula

SERVES 4 AS A MAIN COURSE

I GOT THE INSPIRATION FOR THIS RECIPE FROM MY FRIEND SISSEL KVELLO, THE LONGTIME PROPRIETOR OF THE STYLISH RESTAURANT ACQUA, LOCATED ON OSLO'S WATERFRONT. THE MATCH BETWEEN MUSHROOMS AND MUSSELS IS ONE MADE IN HEAVEN.

2 cups chicken stock

4 pounds mussels, scrubbed under cold running water and debearded

2 tablespoons finely chopped shallots

1 garlic clove, finely chopped

6 tablespoons unsalted butter

Fine sea salt and freshly ground black pepper

3 tablespoons white wine or water

1 pound wild mushrooms, such as chanterelles or porcini, or button mushrooms, trimmed, cleaned and cut into ⅓-inch slices

4 ounces baby arugula, tough stems removed

3 tablespoons finely chopped fresh chives

In a large pot, bring the chicken stock to a boil. Add the mussels (discard any with cracked shells or that did not close when you scrubbed them), cover, and let steam for 6 to 7 minutes, until most of the shells have opened; discard any that did not open. Remove the mussels from the shells and place them in a serving bowl. Mix in the shallots and garlic while the mussels are still hot. Let cool.

Meanwhile, boil the mussel broth for 10 minutes, or until reduced to approximately 1 cup. Turn off the heat. Whisk in 4 tablespoons of the butter; do not allow the sauce to boil again. Season with salt and pepper.

Combine the remaining 2 tablespoons butter and the white wine in a medium saucepan and heat over medium-low heat. Add the mushrooms and cook for 6 to 7 minutes. Stir the mushrooms and broth into the mussels. Stir in the arugula, sprinkle with the chives, and serve.

Serve with lots of bread, or small baked potatoes, to absorb the juices.

SCALLOPS: DANCING IN THE DEEP

Of all mollusks, the scallop is the one that leads the most interesting life. While the oyster and mussel are confined to a still life, attached to a piece of rock—oblivious of a world beyond that of open mouths, and unable to move around if they grow discontented—the scallop is able to take control of its own life. It does so by snapping its upper valve firmly shut with its powerful oversize adductor muscle and thus expelling water through its fan-shaped shell. The jet stream it produces can propel it as far as three feet at a time, making it as mobile as most crustaceans. When it is not jetting around from one place to another looking for adventure, it is demonstrating its freedom to do so by jumping up and down on the sea bank. If you are diving off the coast of Norway, you may be lucky enough to come across a sandbank full of dancing scallops, an unbelievably beautiful underwater ballet.

As is true of most shellfish, the scallop is at its best when harvested from cold waters, making the coast of Norway the perfect breeding ground. A scallop straight out of the cold January waters needs little or no preparation—not even cooking.

In Norway, scallops are always sold in the shell, preferably still alive. They have to be handled very carefully and will keep for only a day or so after they have been harvested.

Most people think of scallops as the shiny white, incredibly tender adductor muscle. This is the only part that is kept when scallops are cleaned at sea. While the rest of the scallop will begin to smell and become inedible within a day or two after it has been harvested, the muscle can be kept for several days without spoiling. However, if you are able to get hold of live scallops, the reward more than makes up for the higher price and the inconvenience of having to clean them yourself. Not only are the shells themselves like beautiful artwork—no wonder Botticelli depicted Venus in a scallop shell—there is a hidden, not-much-used treasure in the shell as well: the orange roe, not unlike the flesh of a lobster claw in appearance, and the most delicious part of the scallop. Its velvety texture and rich, almost oily taste are a sensual contrast to the lean muscle.

Scallop Carpaccio

SERVES 2 AS AN APPETIZER

4 large live scallops in the shell (see headnote)

1 teaspoon honey

2 teaspoons white wine vinegar

About 1½ teaspoons fleur de sel or other flaky sea salt

2 lime wedges (optional)

Check to see if the scallops are alive by holding them under cold running water. They should close firmly within a few seconds. A dead scallop will very soon give off a bad smell; discard it.

You can ask your fishmonger to clean the scallops for you, but as you want them to be as fresh as possible, the best thing is to clean them yourself. With a sharp knife, cut the scallops open: Pressing the knife firmly against the flat half of each shell, cut the adductor muscle. Once you have cut the adductor muscle, the shell will open by itself. Remove the muscle (the scallop) and the orange roe; discard the rest. Gently wash the scallops and the roe under cold running water.

Mix the honey and vinegar in a small warmed bowl (the two will not combine easily if cold).

With a thin sharp knife, cut the scallops horizontally into thin slices. There is no fixed rule as to how thin the slices should be—I try to cut them as thin as possible, but the last two slices always end up thicker than the others.

Spread the slices out on a plate. Place the roe on two plates and make 8 small slits in each one with a sharp knife. Sprinkle each roe with 2 to 3 drops of the honey-vinegar mixture. Drizzle a few flakes of salt over the scallops and serve immediately, with lime, if desired, on the side.

SCALLOPS THAT HAVE JUST TOUCHED THE PAN, SERVED WITH A VELVETY-SMOOTH CELERIAC PUREE AND A RICH VEAL GLACE, ARE A GREAT WINTER DISH THAT CAN BE EITHER A MAIN COURSE OR AN APPETIZER.

Scallops with Cardamom Veal Glace and Celeriac Puree

SERVES 2 AS A MAIN COURSE, 6 AS AN APPETIZER

12 scallops

1 pound celeriac, peeled and cut into 1-inch dice

1 medium potato, peeled and cut into 1-inch dice

1/2 cup whole milk

7 tablespoons unsalted butter

2 cups veal stock, homemade or store-bought

1 bay leaf

1 cardamom pod

5 black peppercorns

1/2 teaspoon grated orange zest

1 tablespoon sugar

Fine sea salt and freshly ground black pepper

Thirty minutes before cooking them, take the scallops out of the refrigerator and place them on a large plate.

To make the celeriac puree, bring a medium pot of water to a boil. Add the celeriac and potato and boil gently for 15 to 20 minutes, until tender. Drain, transfer to a food processor, and puree until smooth.

Return the puree to the pot. Add the milk and bring to a boil over medium-low heat, stirring constantly. Turn off the heat and stir in 3 tablespoons of the butter. Cover loosely to keep warm.

Meanwhile, prepare the veal glace: In a medium saucepan, combine the veal stock, bay leaf, cardamom, and peppercorns and bring to a boil over medium heat. Cook until reduced to 1/4 cup. Stir in the orange zest and let stand for 2 minutes, then strain the glace and discard the solids.

Return the glace to the pan and bring to a boil. Turn off the heat and stir in 2 tablespoons of the butter.

Finally, season the scallops with the sugar and sprinkle generously with salt and pepper. In a large nonstick skillet, heat the remaining 2 tablespoons butter over high heat. Add the scallops and cook for 1 minute; flip and cook for 1 minute on the other side.

Serve the scallops on top of the celeriac puree, with the veal glace spooned over them.

Pepper-Grilled Oysters and Scallops

SERVES 6 AS AN APPETIZER

THIS IS A GREAT-TASTING AND SURPRISINGLY EASY WAY TO GIVE OYSTERS AND SCALLOPS A SMOKY, PEPPERY FLAVOR. THE TECHNIQUE IS SIMPLE YET INGENIOUS: THROW A HANDFUL OF BLACK PEPPERCORNS ON THE GRILL, COVER THE SCALLOPS AND OYSTERS WITH FOIL, AND COOK FOR A COUPLE OF MINUTES, LEAVING THEM WITH A WONDERFUL AND AROMATIC TASTE.

3 tablespoons white wine vinegar

2 teaspoons honey

1 tablespoon Dijon mustard

¼ cup olive oil

12 scallops

12 freshly shucked oysters on the half-shell (with their brine)

Fine sea salt and freshly ground black pepper

1 teaspoon dried thyme

½ cup black peppercorns

1 lemon, cut into 6 wedges

Heat a gas grill to medium-hot, or prepare a medium-hot fire in a charcoal grill.

Combine the vinegar, honey, mustard, and oil in a warmed bowl and whisk together with a fork (heating the bowl makes the honey mix more easily with the other ingredients). Pour half the vinaigrette into a small serving bowl. Set aside. Toss the scallops with the remaining vinaigrette, remove them from the bowl, and season with salt, pepper, and thyme. Season the oysters with pepper only.

The grilling has to be done very quickly. Have a 3-foot-long sheet of aluminum foil ready. Grill the scallops for 30 seconds on one side only. Place the oyster shells on the grill—try to balance them so they don't lose any of their brine. Turn the scallops, throw the black peppercorns onto the hottest part of the fire, cover the shellfish tightly with foil to trap the smoke, and step back. Let the scallops and oysters cook for about 2 minutes, then remove them and serve immediately—the scallops with the remaining vinaigrette, the oysters with the lemon wedges.

I learned the technique from my friend chef-turned-filmmaker Henrik Henriksen. The same method can be used to flavor beef or duck.

When I made this on my television show from the south coast of Norway, my guests were locals who had never tasted oysters before—even though the seabed is full of them. Here the oysters are served with nothing but lemon wedges, the scallops with a simple sweet vinaigrette. Sometimes, when I am more adventurous, I season the oysters with a little garlic and chipotle chile.

I use only scallops and oysters that are fresh enough to be eaten raw. If you are uncertain about the freshness, I suggest you grill them for 2 to 3 more minutes until they are cooked through. I insist on shucking my own oysters to ensure freshness. Use any kind of medium to large oyster— freshness matters more than type.

CRAYFISH: THERE IS SOMETHING CRAWLING IN MY BATHTUB

It is early in the morning, and I am still half asleep as I enter the bathroom to have my refreshing morning shower. With the ungraceful movements of a sleepwalker, I place my left foot in the bathtub, and before I have had time to let the right foot follow suit, I am wide awake, and I remember everything from last night's nocturnal adventure. I am not alone. The bathtub is crawling with fighting black crayfish, one of which has secured a firm and rather painful grip on my little toe.

In Norway, late August brings with it the threat of autumn. The days are markedly shorter, there is a cool current in the air, and the leaves are slowly starting their transformation from bright green to fiery red. But fall also brings with it new and wonderful things. Last night was the first day of the crayfish season. Being a city boy with many things on my mind, I had not really planned for the event, but a small notice in the local newspaper had alerted me that the crayfish swimming in the city river were now free for all. It was a dark and cloudy night with a forecast of rain that never materialized—the perfect conditions for catching

crayfish. I waited until nearly midnight and then drove up to the outskirts of Oslo, where the Akers River runs into town. There, with the city to my right and the Oslo forest to my left, I waded out onto the shallow sandbanks. There is really no secret to crayfish catching, no difficult technique to be learned. Armed with nothing but a bucket and a flashlight, I managed to catch about thirty small crayfish. The crayfish are stunned by the strong light, allowing you to pick them up with your hands. Some do start to swim away, but they do not go more than a few feet.

The crayfish are best kept alive to ensure that they are eaten as fresh as possible. Placing them in the bathtub under a gentle stream of cold running water is the most practical way for those of us who do not have an aquarium. It also gives the crayfish time to empty their intestines, making it possible to eat them without going through the meticulous process of cleaning them. But right now, this morning, I feel that the crayfish, whom, it is true, I had brought into the house, are invading my private space. More than anything else, I want a shower.

I dash into the kitchen, fill a large pot with salted water, and bring it to a boil. Without further ado, I tip the protesting black crayfish into the pot. By the time I am finished showering, they have been transformed from annoying visitors to breakfast, and to underline the transformation, their shining black armor has turned to crimson red. Well showered and dressed, I have a breakfast that will always be in the pantheon of my life's truly great meals: the freshest and sweetest crayfish I have ever tasted, piled on top of white bread and washed down with orange juice, while the lazy August sun caresses my kitchen.

Boiled Crayfish with Dill

SERVES 4

The annual crayfish party is an important event in both Norway and Sweden. This recipe is the Swedish way to prepare crayfish: Cook them in dill-flavored salted water and beer. When I made this dish on *New Scandinavian Cooking,* we were out in the Oslo forest, on one of the remote hiking trails. When we had finished shooting, we gave away samples to passersby. They were slightly puzzled to find a kitchen in the middle of the forest and kept asking what we were selling and whether we had considered going into a more densely populated area.

Serve with quartered lemons and mayonnaise and thinly sliced white bread, if desired.

6 pounds live crayfish or Louisiana crawfish

$2/3$ cup coarse sea salt

3 tablespoons sugar

3 bottles dark beer, preferably an English stout

1 large bunch fresh dill, plus a few sprigs for garnish

Lemon wedges

Mayonnaise and thin slices good white bread (optional)

Put the crayfish in the sink under cold running water to make sure they are alive. Discard any that do not move.

In a large pot, combine 2 gallons cold water, the salt, sugar, beer, and dill and bring to a boil over high heat. Add the crayfish, return to a boil, and turn off the heat. Let stand for an hour or two before serving.

Drain the crayfish and arrange on a large serving platter. Garnish with dill and squeeze some lemon juice over them.

Crack open the shells at the table and carefully remove the crayfish meat. Place the meat on white bread spread with mayonnaise, or eat it just as it is, with a drop of lemon juice. The white meat in the tail is the best, but that from the head is also delicious; do not eat the papery gills.

White Wine–Steamed Crayfish with Chile, Garlic, and Coriander

SERVES 2 AS A MAIN COURSE, 4 AS AN APPETIZER

THIS IS A MORE SPICY CRAYFISH PREPARATION THAN THE PREVIOUS RECIPE. AGAIN IT IS PREFERABLE TO USE LIVE CRAYFISH (SEE MAIL-ORDER SOURCES, PAGE 294). IF YOU CANNOT FIND LIVE CRAYFISH, YOU CAN FRY THAWED FROZEN CRAYFISH QUICKLY IN THE OIL AND THE SPICES, THEN SERVE THEM.

IF YOU WANT TO DOUBLE THE AMOUNT OF CRAYFISH, YOU DO NOT NEED TO DOUBLE THE AMOUNT OF OIL, SPICES, AND WINE; COOK THE CRAYFISH IN TWO BATCHES.

3 pounds live crayfish or Louisiana crawfish

1/2 cup olive oil

4 garlic cloves, chopped

2 tablespoons coriander seeds, lightly crushed

1 red chile pepper, seeded and chopped

1 tablespoon salt

One 750-ml bottle dry white wine

1/2 cup finely chopped fresh dill

4 tablespoons unsalted butter

Mayonnaise and thin slices good white bread (optional)

Lemon wedges for garnish

Put the crayfish under cold running water to make sure they are alive. Discard any that do not move.

Heat the oil in a large pot over high heat. Add the garlic, coriander, chile, crayfish, and salt and sauté for 3 to 4 minutes, until the crayfish are starting to turn red. Add the wine, place a tight-fitting lid on the pot, and let the crayfish steam for 10 minutes. Remove the lid and toss the crayfish around with a wooden spoon. Place the lid back on and steam for an additional 10 minutes. Transfer the crayfish to a large serving bowl or platter and sprinkle with the dill.

Strain the broth and discard the solids. Return the broth to the pot, bring it to a boil, and cook, uncovered, until reduced to about 2 cups. Stir in the butter and pour over the crayfish. Serve immediately.

Break open the shells at the table and carefully remove the crayfish meat. Place the meat on white bread spread with mayonnaise, or simply dip it in the cooking juices and a squeeze of lemon. The white meat in the tail is the best, but that from the head is also delicious; do not eat the papery gills.

Serve with mayonnaise, dill, and lots of bread to sop up the juices.

LOBSTER: COFFEE AND CAVIAR

It is not yet 7 A.M. and still dark when fisherman Terje Bernhardsen arrives at the deserted docks on his curious-looking three-wheel moped. His tiny trailer is full of half-rotten fish, and after a few minutes the cold winter air smells like a bustling fishing port in the tropics. The smell awakens the seagulls, which raise a commotion—a cacophony that is bound to wake up anyone still asleep in the surrounding Norwegian fishing village of Ula.

Bernhardsen is one of the last professional lobster fishermen left in the Oslo fjord, an hour's drive from the capital. The smelly fish is an unpleasant necessity in his line of work.

Whenever he has some time on his hands, he fishes for anything he can get, normally pollock, haddock, mackerel, and small cod. Then he leaves them out in his garage for a few days before using them as bait for the lobster pots. If he used fresh fish in the lobster pots, they would be filled with crabs. But with rotten fish, only the valuable and strangely undiscriminating lobsters dare approach.

It is going to be a beautiful winter day. The sun is not yet up, and as we head out to the lobster pots in Bernhardsen's boat *Irene II,* it feels as if we have the world to ourselves. We huddle together and scout for the bright orange buoys marking the whereabouts of the lobster pots.

The first lobster pot is empty. My heart sinks. The second is also empty. I suddenly feel tired and cold. Then our luck turns. In the third pot there is a nice four-pound lobster and a two-pound relative. And there are more to come. After hoisting seven pots, we have nearly a case full of shiny black lobsters.

"People complain that the lobsters are dying out, but I cannot see that there has been much of a change since I started fishing forty years ago," says Bernhardsen. "The lobsters are hard to catch—they always have been. In order to find them, you need to know their whereabouts, and you need to invest a lot of time. People don't have that time anymore, and therefore they assume that the lobster is dying out."

The lobsters in the case have recovered from the first shock of being abducted from their natural environment, and they are now following their aggressive instincts. The big lobsters are trying to kill the small ones. The small ones are trying to kill the even smaller ones. The smallest ones are putting up a fight as well, but they are losing. Bernhardsen breaks up the fight and gently, like a caring father, places a wet piece of cloth over them, more precisely an old shirt, just like the one he is wearing. After a few seconds, the lobsters start moving less and less, until it looks as if they are sleeping.

Lobsters are rare and expensive all over the world, but nowhere more so than in northern Europe. The northern European lobster is a different species from the ones that live off the North American coast. It is more territorial, which makes reproduction more difficult. In addition, it has a slower growth rate.

The morning fog has cleared and the sun is looking at us from afar, giving away just enough energy to thaw us out. "This one is too small," says Bernhardsen, and holds out a lobster that does not fulfill the minimum requirement of ten inches.

"But if you see here, she is full of roe." The underside of the tail is full of glistening black roe. Thousands of shiny black eggs—a promise of lobsters to come. She is released back into the sea.

I am exhausted from the laborious work of hoisting the lobster pots, and we break for coffee. Bernhardsen offers dry crackers and hot coffee in large mugs. Then he moves the wet shirt covering the lobsters, lifts up a female, and implores me to sample the roe.

"She can't feel it, you know. Don't be afraid. It is delicious. Most people just throw the roe away."

Out on the open sea, with its long, quiet swells, fresh air, and a sun that reminds you that winter isn't all bad, the roe tastes better than any caviar I have ever eaten. The thin coffee tastes better than any Champagne. I take another cracker with fresh lobster roe, fill up my coffee mug, and rest my head against the railing. Slowly sipping my coffee I notice the inscription on the plastic mug: *"Navigare vivere est"*—"Sailing is living." I couldn't agree more.

Tarragon Lobster with Asparagus

SERVES 2

THIS IS A SIMPLE RECIPE THAT MAKES THE MOST OF ONE LOBSTER. THE LOBSTER IS COOKED IN ITS OWN JUICES, WHITE WINE, AND BUTTER. THIS PRESERVES MORE OF THE FLAVORS AND, BECAUSE IT IS RICH, MAKES IT POSSIBLE TO SERVE SMALLER PORTIONS.

One live 3-pound lobster

8 tablespoons (1 stick) unsalted butter

1 garlic clove, finely chopped

2 tablespoons chopped shallots

1½ cups dry white wine

1 tablespoon chopped fresh tarragon, or 1 teaspoon dried tarragon plus 1 teaspoon tarragon vinegar

1 pound asparagus, trimmed

¼ teaspoon curry powder

Fine sea salt

Kill the lobster, preferably with a butcher knife through the head (this has been proven to be the most humane way of killing crustaceans): Holding the lobster on a cutting board, plunge the knife into the head. Then pull the knife down and forward, splitting the front of the head in two; this kills the lobster instantly. Or plunge the lobster into a large pot of boiling water for 1 minute. Cut the lobster lengthwise in half; make sure to save all the juices released from the lobster. Crack the claw shells.

Heat 2 tablespoons of the butter in a large skillet over medium heat. Sauté the garlic and shallots for 3 to 4 minutes, until soft. Add the lobster to the pan and sauté for 4 to 5 minutes. Pour over the white wine and the reserved lobster juices, sprinkle with most of the tarragon, cover, and simmer for 15 minutes.

Transfer the lobster to a warm serving platter. Turn the heat up, add the asparagus, and cook for 7 minutes, until the cooking juices are reduced by half and the asparagus is still crisp. Season with curry powder, salt, and the rest of the tarragon. Stir in the remaining 6 tablespoons butter and let it melt, then pour the sauce over the lobster and serve the asparagus alongside.

Serve lots of bread to sop up the buttery cooking juices.

Crab Cocktail
with Dill and Mint

SERVES 6 TO 8 AS AN APPETIZER

$2/3$ cup mayonnaise

3 tablespoons fresh lemon juice

2 teaspoons sugar

2 tablespoons finely chopped
fresh dill

$1/2$ cup heavy (whipping) cream

2 pounds cooked crabmeat

6 to 8 thin lemon slices for garnish

24 fresh mint leaves for garnish

In a bowl, mix the mayonnaise, lemon juice, sugar, and dill. In a separate bowl, whip the cream until stiff. Gently fold the whipped cream into the mayonnaise mixture.

Layer the crabmeat and cream in martini glasses or bowls. Garnish each one with a slice of lemon and a few mint leaves, then serve.

Crab Cakes with Parsley, Mustard, and Parmesan

SERVES 2 AS A MAIN COURSE, 4 AS AN APPETIZER

THESE CRAB CAKES ARE SOFT AND DELICIOUS. A MORE TRADITIONAL WAY TO MAKE THEM WOULD BE TO USE EGGS, NOT PARMESAN, TO HOLD THE CAKES TOGETHER. I LIKE THE WAY THE PARMESAN ADDS AN INTERESTING FLAVOR TO THE CRAB CAKES, BUT THEY WILL BE MORE DELICATE TO WORK WITH.

1 pound freshly cooked crabmeat, well drained

¼ cup finely chopped fresh parsley

2 tablespoons Dijon-style mustard

½ cup freshly grated Parmesan

¼ cup bread crumbs

2 tablespoons all-purpose flour, or more if needed

3 tablespoons fresh lemon juice

1 large egg (optional)

2 tablespoons unsalted butter

Small sprigs fresh dill or basil for garnish

Lemon wedges for garnish

In a medium bowl, combine all of the ingredients except the butter and garnishes, mixing gently until you have a firm mixture. If the mixture is too liquid, add more flour.

Heat the butter in a large nonstick skillet over medium heat. Working in batches, using your fingers and a spoon, mold the crabmeat mixture into 12 small cakes and add to the skillet, making sure you do not crowd the pan. Cook for 4 minutes, carefully flip the cakes, and cook for 3 more minutes. Transfer to a serving plate and repeat until all the crab mixture is used up.

Garnish with the dill and lemon wedges. Serve warm.

Serve with Cucumber Salad (page 85) or Green Beans and Peas with Celeriac and Mango (page 230), and sour cream or Yogurt-Mint Sauce (page 165).

8

SHEEP IN BLACK TIE AND STOCKINGS

Once every year I drop everything else and go hunting on the unsheltered, inhospitable islands of the Austevoll archipelago in western Norway. It is a beautiful and exhausting hunt that features no guns and no traps, where we, the hunters, are armed with nothing but nylon stockings and unfashionable company neckties. With these somewhat unorthodox weapons, we wage a battle to conquer one of the bravest and most hardy animals—the wild sheep, a special breed of sheep with large horns and exceptional athletic abilities that thrives under extreme conditions.

The wild sheep are an example of nature's ability to perform magic— to get something out of almost nothing. They live by themselves, roam around the islands freely, and feed on whatever they can find of heather, grass, and small shrubs. Even in the winter, when the climate can be hostile, to say the least, the sheep stay outside, staring out into the Atlantic—waiting patiently for better times. They are never fed anything and must subsist on what they can find in their remote territories. When food is scarce, or when snow makes it inaccessible, they head down to the beach to feed on seaweed and kelp.

The meat of the wild sheep is juicier and better tasting than any meat I have ever experienced—with a rich gamy flavor that bears witness to a life unaffected by modern industrialized agriculture. Even though sheep have been domesticated for several thousand years, and the sheep on Austevoll have owners' tags attached to their ears, their lives do not differ much from what they were when all sheep were wild. They even shed their own wool, unlike the domesticated sheep that have to be sheared.

The wild sheep come in contact with humans only once a year, at the annual sheep gathering, or "sheep hunt," as it is commonly referred to. One day in October, all the people of Austevoll—business executives, teachers,

engineers, farmers, and fishermen alike—come together to help each other gather the sheep, count their livestock, and pick out lambs to be slaughtered. It is a great experience, and one I never miss. For a few hours it is man against sheep, in an unarmed standoff that nearly always leads to the victory of man. But the beauty of it is that at times it seems as if the sheep have the upper hand.

Nowhere is the battle more magnificent than on the island of Fugløy, one of the westernmost islands of the Austevoll archipelago. The 250-acre island faces straight out into the open sea—if you set

off going west, the next stop will be North America. There are no trees to give shelter, and hardly any grass—just heather, moss, and rocks. Up until the early 1960s, the island was inhabited by a dozen people, stubbornly insisting on their right to live on the outskirts of civilization. But in 1962 a powerful storm blew all the boathouses into the ocean. When the inhabitants woke up to the sight of nothingness where boats, fishing nets, and lobster pots had been, it was as if their stubbornness had been blown away, too. Shortly thereafter, they

started to dismantle their houses and moved to the mainland. The only remaining living beings were one hundred or so wild sheep.

The first part of the sheep hunt is calm and pleasant. After a temporary enclosure has been set up on the small field on the north side of the island, where the houses used to stand, a group of about thirty of us, men and women, walks across the island in fan formation, making a human wall, pushing the shy sheep over to the relatively flat terrain near the eastern tip of the island. The rams—all sporting majestic, curved horns—are not so easily intimidated and alternate between trying to scare us away and running to elude capture.

When all the sheep have gathered in a relatively concentrated area, the real chase begins. A smaller group of young athletic men and women—the runners—approach the sheep from the south side, pushing them north toward a small ridge that will lead them straight into the enclosure. But it is never that easy: Once the sheep start running, it is hard to follow. If one of us lags behind and the sheep are able to find a big enough gap in our human wall, they will make a run for it. Some make a jump for the sea and one of us must wade out to catch them; some use their horns to fight their way out of trouble. There have been episodes where people have been rammed hard in sensitive places.

After about an hour of running, stumbling, shouting, and cursing, most of the sheep are safely jammed together in the enclosure.

Some years we don't succeed, though, and we are left with fewer than twenty animals. Even in good years, at least a dozen get away. A few even manage to jump the five-foot fence of the enclosure. We don't even try to go after those. They have earned their right to freedom.

Exhausted and happy, we break for lunch—appropriately enough, a traditional lamb stew called lamb in cabbage, a miracle of a three-ingredient dish: Lamb, cabbage, and whole black peppercorns are cooked over low heat for several hours, until the cabbage has turned sweet, the flavors of the lamb have doubled or quadrupled in intensity, and the peppercorns have added a wonderfully rich and spicy flavor.

Reinvigorated by the hearty meal, we set off on the last phase of the adventure. The sheep are counted and those that are going to be returned to nature are tagged. For a few minutes, they

seem subdued, even tamed, and the children come over to pat them and see if they recognize any from last year. When they are finally let loose, they greet freedom with an explosion of energy, and after a few giant leaps, they are back on their home turf. It will be another year until they see a human being.

Those that are destined to the mainland are then subjected to the strangest ritual I have yet come across: On their way down to the waiting boats, their feet are tied together. This is done not with rope or string, but with discarded neckties and nylon stockings. Gently, the proud wild animals are incapacitated by two of the most powerful symbols of modern civilization and conformity.

A young ram looks up at me. His horns are not yet fully grown but impressive enough. His eyes show neither pleading nor fear, but still stubborn resilience. He is nevertheless a comic sight, for his legs are tied up with a pair of beige nylon stockings. The ewe

next to him is sporting a 1980s-style company tie—a gift from the Norwegian Farmers Union.

At first I assume the ties and stockings were used to symbolize the superiority of the human culture, or to signify that the animals were being taken to civilization as the property of the humans. How strange that anthropologists have not reflected upon this beautiful rite of passage, I thought. Especially when you take into consideration that the people here almost always dress casually; except for weddings and funerals, I have hardly seen an islander wear a tie. But when I ask, my speculative theory falls apart, and the answer is as sensible and down to earth as the people of western Norway: Rope and string would hurt the animals. Nylon stockings and ties—especially cheap company ties made of synthetic materials— are elastic and thus the most comfortable for the animals.

Lamb and Cabbage Stew

SERVES 8 TO 10

This dish is said to be better every time you reheat it. The nineteenth-century Norwegian cookbook writer Olaug Lauken claimed it was best the seventh time around.

Maybe seven is pushing it a bit, but this is definitely a dish that you can make the day before and reheat right before your guests arrive, or make it ahead and freeze it for later.

Because lamb and cabbage stew is a western Norwegian specialty, I made it the first time for the sheep gatherers on Austevoll, while shooting an episode of *New Scandinavian Cooking*. I was nervous about whether they would approve of my way of making it. Luckily, they did.

Serve with boiled potatoes or good bread.

6 pounds bone-in lamb shoulder, trimmed of excess fat and cut into approximately 1$\frac{1}{2}$-inch pieces

4 pounds green cabbage (1$\frac{1}{2}$ heads), shredded

1 to 2 tablespoons black peppercorns

2 bay leaves

3 tablespoons unsalted butter

1 tablespoon all-purpose flour

4 cups cold water

Fine sea salt

Layer the meat and cabbage in a large pot. Add 1 tablespoon of the black peppercorns, the bay leaves, and butter. Sprinkle with the flour and add the water. Cover and slowly bring to a boil over medium-low heat. Cook for 2 hours over low to medium-low heat, until the meat is very tender and the cabbage is soft. If you want the stew to be a bit spicier, add 1 more tablespoon black peppercorns and cook for another 15 minutes. Season with salt to taste.

Remove the bay leaves and serve the stew in the pot or a deep serving dish.

Glazed Leg of Lamb with Roasted Root Vegetables

SERVES 8

If you do not want to risk keeping your guests waiting, you can start cooking the lamb early. Leaving the meat to rest in a warm (120°F) oven after it is cooked only makes it more tender, without fear of overcooking it. (If you have a meat thermometer, use it to check the temperature of the roast, or use an instant-read thermometer.)

The ingredients listed here are only a starting point. Use whatever root vegetables are in season. When baked for a long time and soaked in the beer, stock, and the roasting juices from the lamb, they become wonderfully sweet and delicious, and there is no need for a sauce.

This is one of the crew's favorites from *New Scandinavian Cooking.*

One 6-pound leg of lamb

1 pound parsnips, peeled and cut into approximately 1½-inch pieces

1 pound rutabaga, peeled and cut into approximately 1½-inch pieces

1 pound onions, quartered

1 to 2 pounds russet potatoes, quartered

1 pound carrots, peeled and cut into approximately 1½-inch pieces

2 plump heads garlic, separated into cloves but not peeled

1 cup beer (pilsner type), or more as needed

1 cup lamb, veal, or chicken stock, or more as needed

¼ cup olive oil

2 tablespoons chopped fresh rosemary

Fine sea salt

¼ cup sweet honey mustard, preferably Swedish (see Mail-Order Sources, page 294), or 3 tablespoons Dijon mustard plus 1 tablespoon honey

Let the meat stand at room temperature for 2 hours before roasting. (It is easier to get good, even results when the meat is not cold.)

Preheat the oven to 400°F.

Place all the vegetables in a roasting pan. Place the garlic cloves in among the vegetables. Pour the beer, stock, and olive oil over the vegetables. Sprinkle with the rosemary and season with salt.

Pat the meat dry with paper towels. Rub it all over with 1 tablespoon salt. If not using honey mustard, combine the Dijon mustard and honey in a small bowl. Rub the leg with the honey mustard or mustard-and-honey mixture. Place a meat thermometer, if you have one, in the thickest part of the leg; make sure it does not touch the bone.

Place the leg of lamb on a rack that will fit over the roasting pan. Place the roasting pan on the bottom rack of the oven and set the rack with the lamb over the pan, so the roasting juices will drip down onto the vegetables. Cook for 15 minutes, then reduce the heat to 350°F. Cook for another 1½ hours, or until the meat thermometer (or an instant-read thermometer) reads 145°F. Make sure the vegetables do not dry; if they look dry, add another cup or so of beer or stock.

Let the meat rest, uncovered, on a carving board for at least 30 minutes. Leave the vegetables in the oven to keep warm.

When the meat is ready, transfer the vegetables to a serving platter. I like to carve the meat at the table, but you may choose to carve it in the kitchen; make sure the serving platter is warm (but not hot). The muscle fibers on a leg of lamb run more or less parallel with the bone. For a more tender texture, slice the meat across the muscle fibers. Serve the lamb with the root vegetables; be sure to squeeze the softened garlic out of the skins and spread it on the meat as you eat.

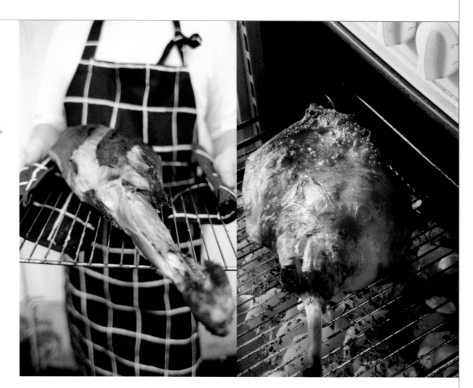

Rosemary-and-Garlic-Marinated Leg of Lamb with Roasted Garlic

SERVES 8

Serve with Brussels Sprouts with Lemon and Parsley (page 234) and Potato Gratin with Parsnips and Rutabaga (page 72), or just the roasted root vegetables from the recipe for Glazed Leg of Lamb (page 160).

One 6-pound bone-in leg of lamb

2 tablespoons fine sea salt

¼ cup finely chopped fresh rosemary

5 garlic cloves, minced

½ cup olive oil

3 tablespoons fresh lemon juice

8 heads of garlic

Rub the leg of lamb with the salt. In a food processor, combine the rosemary, garlic, olive oil, and lemon juice and pulse until you have a smooth puree. Press the rosemary mixture through a metal sieve with the back of a spoon. Place the lamb in a baking dish and pour the marinade over. Let marinate overnight. Let stand at room temperature for 2 hours before roasting. (It is easier to get good, even results when the meat is not cold.)

Preheat the oven to 400°F.

To roast, insert a meat thermometer, if you have one, into the thickest part of the meat; make sure it does not touch the bone. Place the leg of lamb in a roasting pan and roast in the middle of the oven for 15 minutes. Reduce the heat to 350°F and place the heads of garlic around the meat. Roast for 1 hour and 15 minutes, or until the meat thermometer (or an instant-read thermometer) registers 145°F. Transfer the meat to a carving board and let rest, uncovered, for at least 30 minutes. Turn off the oven and leave the garlic inside to keep warm.

Cut the heads of garlic in half with a sharp knife. Carve the meat and place it on a large warm serving platter, along with the garlic. Serve immediately, providing a small spoon for each person to scoop out the roasted garlic.

Dill-and-Fennel Stewed Lamb

SERVES 6

DILL IS A CLOSE RELATIVE OF FENNEL AND WHEN COOKED TOGETHER LIKE THIS THE TWO BECOME VIRTUALLY INDISTINGUISHABLE. IF YOU CANNOT FIND UNSALTED VEGETABLE STOCK, USE LIGHTLY SALTED STOCK AND REDUCE THE AMOUNT OF SALT ACCORDINGLY.

4 pounds boneless lamb leg or shoulder, cut into 1-inch pieces

6 cups unsalted vegetable stock

1 bay leaf

10 white peppercorns

8 stalks fresh dill tied together with cotton string, plus 1 cup chopped fresh dill

Fine sea salt

1 large fennel bulb, trimmed and cut into 1½-inch pieces

1 tablespoon white wine vinegar, or more to taste

1 teaspoon sugar

1 tablespoon cornstarch or all-purpose flour

Freshly ground white pepper

Fill a large pot with about 2 quarts water and bring to a boil over high heat. Blanch the meat for 2 minutes. Drain and rinse the meat under cold running water; rinse out the pot. (This first step ensures a clearer stock, but it can be skipped, without much compromise of flavor, if you are in a hurry.)

Add the vegetable stock to the pot and bring to a boil over medium-high heat. Add the meat, return to a boil, and skim off the foam that forms on the surface with a large spoon. Add the bay leaf, white peppercorns, dill stalks, and salt. Reduce the heat and simmer gently for 1 hour, skimming the foam or fat from time to time.

Add the fennel and continue cooking for 15 minutes. Remove the meat and fennel with a slotted spoon and transfer to a bowl.

Strain the stock, discard the solids, and return the stock to the pot. Bring to a boil over medium heat and cook until reduced to approximately 2 cups. Add the vinegar and sugar. In a small bowl, mix the cornstarch with 2 tablespoons cold water until smooth; make sure there are no lumps. Gradually stir half the cornstarch mixture into the stock and bring to a boil over medium-low heat; if you would like the stock thicker, add more of the cornstarch mixture. Add the meat and fennel, stir in the chopped dill, and cook for about 4 minutes. Season with salt and pepper to taste, and more vinegar, if necessary. Serve immediately.

Nowhere is dill more popular than in Sweden, where it is used not only to flavor fish and salads, but frequently with meat as well. Dill-stewed lamb is a traditional Swedish dish. This recipe, inspired by Swedish food writer and restaurateur Carl Butler, is more modern and lighter tasting than the traditional version.

Serve with Potatoes with Goose Fat and Lemon (page 74).

In Scandinavia, lamb and mushrooms are two of the best flavors of autumn. The addition of the wonderful freshness of mint makes this a delicious way to serve lamb chops. This recipe is excellent for grilling, as well. Prepare the mushrooms and zucchini in advance, and grill the lamb chops separately.

Lamb Chops with Mushrooms, Zucchini, and Yogurt-Mint Sauce

SERVES 4

If you cannot find chanterelles or other wild mushrooms, you can obtain some of the same wonderful depth of flavor by sprinkling the cultivated mushrooms with a little bit of dried porcini or other dried wild mushrooms.

The garlic should be absolutely fresh and have no trace of green shoots. These shoots are an indication that the garlic has become somewhat bitter, and it will be much too strong for the mushrooms.

Serve with Green Pea Puree with Asparagus and Scallions (page 227) or Onion Pie with Jarlsberg and Thyme (page 223).

8 small lamb rib chops (about 2 pounds total)

Fine sea salt and freshly ground black pepper

18 to 20 fresh mint leaves, plus (optional) chopped mint for garnish

1 tablespoon unsalted butter

1 plump garlic clove, crushed

1 pound mixed wild mushrooms, trimmed, cleaned, and cut into 1/3-inch slices, or 1 pound button mushrooms, trimmed, cleaned, and sliced, plus 1 ounce dried wild mushrooms, rinsed

3 to 4 tablespoons Cognac or other brandy

3 tablespoons olive oil

2 small zucchini, quartered lengthwise and cut into 2-inch pieces

Yogurt-Mint Sauce (recipe follows)

Season the lamb chops with salt and pepper. Crush half the mint leaves gently, then chop and sprinkle over the lamb chops.

Melt the butter in a saucepan. Sauté the garlic for 2 minutes, then add the mushrooms (including the dried mushrooms, if you are using them) and cook for 5 minutes. Add the brandy and the remaining mint leaves and cook for another 5 minutes over low heat. Remove from the heat and cover to keep warm.

Heat the olive oil in a large skillet over high heat. Cook the lamb chops for 1 minute on each side, then transfer to a plate to rest. Add the zucchini to the skillet and cook, stirring, for 3 minutes, until slightly tender. Transfer to a plate.

Reduce the heat under the pan to medium, return the lamb chops to the pan, and cook for an additional 2 minutes on each side. Transfer to a serving plate. Quickly reheat the zucchini in the pan; reheat the mushrooms if necessary.

Serve the lamb, sprinkled with more fresh mint if you like, with Yogurt-Mint Sauce.

Yogurt-Mint Sauce

MAKES 1 CUP

**1 tablespoon finely chopped
fresh mint leaves**

¹⁄₂ teaspoon coarse sea salt

2 tablespoons fresh lemon juice

1 teaspoon sugar

1 cup plain yogurt

Freshly ground black pepper

Place the mint in a mortar or a small bowl. Add the salt and lightly crush the mint and salt with a pestle or the back of a wooden spoon. Add the lemon juice, sugar, and yogurt. Season with pepper to taste. (The sauce can be made up to 24 hours in advance; cover and refrigerate.)

A delicious sauce that goes well with all kinds of lamb dishes, this is also excellent as a dip with vegetables.

9

THE FIRST VANGUARD

Hulda Garborg was one of the most influential Norwegian women's activists of the 1890s, and the wife of author and social reformer Arne Garborg. The couple was among the first Norwegian members of the European intellectual vanguard. They traveled widely on the Continent, partaking of bohemian life. At home they advocated modern causes such as women's rights and free love. They criticized the authority of the church and embraced socialism and, in its turn, anarchism—then they distanced themselves from both when the doctrines became too dogmatic. At the same time, they were instrumental in the dawning nationalist movement, as champions for Norwegian independence and self-awareness.

It was as a part of this struggle that Hulda published her cookbook *Heimstell (Housekeeping)* in 1898. Her aim was to encourage Norwegians, especially those living in the rural areas, to take pride in their own food traditions and not just copy the urban elite's French- and Danish-inspired bourgeois cuisine, which Hulda found insipid and unsuitable for Norway.

Heimstell is one of the first truly Norwegian cookbooks and an interesting example of two important trends in Norwegian cultural life: nationalism and internationalism. Because of our long history of being governed by our neighbors, first by Denmark from the fifteenth century to 1814, and then as the junior partner in a union with Sweden until 1905, these two seemingly conflicting ideologies have often appeared together. Both building national identity and linking up with the broader international society were seen as ways of opposing the semicolonial rulers in Stockholm and Copenhagen.

But there was one major obstacle in the making of Hulda the cookbook author: She couldn't cook. When Hulda married Arne in 1887, she admitted, "I do not know

how to make *any* kind of food." Among friends she had a reputation for being an exceptionally bad cook. So when, in the early 1890s, she started to write a food column in a newspaper, it was considered a joke by many. But while most cookbook writers at the time were copying prestigious French books, addressing an almost nonexistent elite and giving advice on how to entertain in grand style ("If the sauce breaks, beat in 20 more egg yolks and have the maid beat

the sauce energetically for another 45 minutes," says one classic nineteenth-century cookbook), Hulda's relative inexperience served as an advantage. She acknowledged her own weaknesses and, unlike her colleagues, she actually researched her writing. She talked to people about what they considered to be good Norwegian food, she interviewed peasant wives to find out how they made their regional

specialties, and she tried to re-create the simple, good food she had been served on her journeys, especially to France.

"I feel passionately that we, in cooking as in everything else, must build on our own traditions. Build on our own traditions, and from there expand our view and our knowledge," she wrote in 1925, toward the end of her life. Despite her own faults as a cook, her influence in defining Norwegian food is indisputable.

Vodka-Marinated Sirloin

SERVES 8

THE FINE, ALMOST EPHEMERAL TASTE OF VODKA IS EXCELLENT TO USE IN MARINADES. IT IS A WONDERFUL MEDIUM FOR OTHER FLAVORS, IN THIS CASE PARSLEY, THYME, GARLIC, SALT, AND CRUSHED BLACK PEPPER.

IN ORDER FOR THE MARINADE TO PENETRATE THE MEAT, YOU SHOULD LET IT MARINATE IN THE FRIDGE FOR 2 TO 3 DAYS. (IF YOU DO NOT HAVE THAT MUCH TIME, LET IT MARINATE FOR 2 TO 3 HOURS AT ROOM TEMPERATURE.)

One 4-pound boneless sirloin roast or beef tenderloin roast

1 tablespoon coarse sea salt

2 tablespoons crushed black peppercorns

3 tablespoons finely chopped fresh parsley

2 tablespoons plus 1 teaspoon finely chopped fresh thyme

3 garlic cloves, crushed

1/3 cup grain vodka

1/4 cup olive oil

2 tablespoons vegetable oil

4 tablespoons unsalted butter

Rub the roast with the salt and pepper. Place it in a resealable plastic bag. Add the parsley, 2 tablespoons of thyme, and the garlic and pour in the vodka and olive oil. Seal the bag and place it in a bowl in the refrigerator for 2 to 3 days, turning the bag twice a day so the meat marinates evenly.

Let the meat stand at room temperature for 1 to 2 hours before cooking.

Preheat the oven to 425°F.

Take the meat out of the plastic bag; reserve the marinade. Heat a large nonstick skillet over high heat. Add the vegetable oil and heat until hot. Sear the roast on all sides, about 4 to 6 minutes.

Transfer the meat to a baking pan. Place a meat thermometer in the thickest part of the roast. Roast in the middle of the oven, turning once, for 1 to 1¼ hours (25 to 30 minutes if using tenderloin), until the thermometer (or an instant-read thermometer) registers 130°F for medium-rare; before the roast is done, pour the reserved marinade over it. Transfer the meat to a cutting board and let it rest, uncovered, for at least 20 minutes. Set the baking dish aside.

Just before serving, pour the cooking juices into a saucepan and heat gently. Stir in the butter. Season with salt and pepper and the remaining thyme. Strain the sauce and discard the herbs.

Carve the meat and arrange on a platter with the sauce on the side.

This dish was featured on *New Scandinavian Cooking* when we filmed in Svalbard, an Arctic island in the polar ice to the north of northern Norway. The vodka was the only thing that did not freeze on the way to the university where I did the cooking.

Serve with Oven-Dried Tomatoes (page 240), Potato Gratin with Parsnips and Rutabaga (page 72), and Savoy Cabbage with Dill Butter and Bacon (page 237).

Veal Roulades with Leek and Basil

SERVES 4

2 large eggs

2 pounds finely ground veal

2 potatoes, boiled, peeled, and mashed

¼ cup bread crumbs

¼ cup finely chopped onion

½ cup heavy (whipping) cream

Fine sea salt and freshly ground black pepper

¼ cup chopped fresh basil

1 leek, white part only, sliced paper thin

6 tablespoons unsalted butter, melted (optional)

Sour cream for serving

In a large bowl, lightly beat the eggs. Add the meat, potatoes, bread crumbs, onion, and cream. Mix well and season with salt and pepper. Cover and refrigerate for at least 1 hour.

Preheat the oven to 350°F.

Brush a large cutting board with water. With a moist rolling pin, roll out the meat mixture into a rectangle until about ¼ inch thick. Cut into eight 4-inch squares. Place a thin layer of basil and leek on each square. Roll up the squares—you may need the help of a knife or a spatula.

Place the roulades in a baking dish; make sure that there is at least a ½-inch space between each roulade. Brush with the butter, if desired. Bake in the middle of the oven for 20 minutes. Turn the oven to broil and broil for 5 minutes, until lightly browned.

Serve with the sour cream on the side.

Serve with New Potato Salad with Herbs and Green Beans (page 77).

FOR BEST RESULTS, MARINATE THE BEEF FOR 2 TO 3 DAYS IN ORDER TO LET THE FLAVORS OF THE GINGER AND GARLIC PENETRATE. BUT IF YOU DON'T HAVE TIME TO WAIT THAT LONG, A COUPLE OF HOURS WILL DO. THE PROCESS OF ROASTING, THEN RESTING, AND THEN CONTINUING TO ROAST YIELDS VERY JUICY AND TENDER MEAT THAT IS ASTONISHINGLY UNIFORMLY COOKED. AS ALWAYS WITH ROASTING MEAT, THE COOKING TIME VARIES. YOU WILL BENEFIT FROM USING A GOOD MEAT (OR INSTANT-READ) THERMOMETER.

Roast Beef with Garlic and Ginger

SERVES 8

This is a recipe inspired by the book *I Hulda's Kjøkken (In Hulda's Kitchen),* by Ruth Hege Holst. Her book features new interpretations of recipes from Hulda Garborg's 1898 classic *Heimstell (Housekeeping).*

I featured this dish on one episode of *New Scandinavian Cooking;* I cooked outside on one of the islands in the Oslo fjord. Instead of slow-cooking the roast beef, I grilled it.

Serve with Potato Gratin with Parsnips and Rutabaga (page 72) and Broccoli with Capers, Garlic, and Anchovies (page 231). This dish tastes just as good served cold the next day.

One 4-pound beef tenderloin roast or boneless sirloin roast, if preferred

About 2 teaspoons crushed black peppercorns (see Note)

3 tablespoons grated ginger, or more to taste

4 garlic cloves, crushed

1/2 cup olive oil

1/2 cup soy sauce

2 tablespoons fresh lemon juice or 1/4 cup dry white wine, or more to taste

2 tablespoons finely chopped mixed fresh herbs, such as thyme, rosemary, parsley, and/or sage, or more if desired

Fine sea salt and freshly ground black pepper

3 tablespoons unsalted butter, at room temperature

Rub the roast with the pepper. Place the meat in a resealable plastic bag.

To prepare the marinade, combine the ginger, garlic, oil, soy sauce, lemon juice, and herbs in a bowl. Mix well and pour the marinade into the plastic bag. Remove most of the air from the bag and seal it carefully. Place the meat in a bowl (in case the bag leaks) and set it in the refrigerator for 2 to 3 days, turning the bag twice a day so the meat is evenly marinated. (If you're pressed for time, marinate the meat at room temperature for 2 to 3 hours, turning it occasionally.)

Let the meat stand at room temperature for 1 to 2 hours before roasting it. (It is easier to get good, even results when the meat is not cold.)

Preheat the oven to 350°F.

Remove the roast from the bag; set the marinade aside. Scrape the seasonings off the roast with a spoon or a butter knife (as the ginger and garlic are likely to burn during the searing and the first roasting). Rub the roast with salt, pepper, and about 1 tablespoon of the butter.

Heat a large nonstick skillet over high heat. Sear the roast on all sides until browned; this should take about 4 minutes.

Transfer the roast to a baking pan. Place a meat thermometer, if you have one, in the middle of the roast. Roast in the middle of the oven for

40 minutes. Take the roast out of the oven, turn it over, and let it rest, uncovered, for 20 minutes. Reduce the oven temperature to 300°F.

Pour the reserved marinade over the roast and roast for an additional 20 to 30 minutes, or until the thermometer (or an instant-read thermometer) registers 135°F for medium-rare, 145°F for medium. Transfer the meat to a cutting board and let it rest, uncovered, for at least 20 minutes. (If you keep the meat thermometer in the roast, you will notice that the temperature increases a few degrees, and then very slowly starts to decrease.) Set the baking dish aside.

Just before serving, pour the pan juices and any juices that have collected on the carving board into a small saucepan and simmer for 2 minutes. Strain the liquid through a metal sieve lined with a piece of cheesecloth and return it to the pan. Season with lemon juice, salt, and/or ginger, if necessary. Stir in the rest of the butter; do not let the sauce boil.

Carve the meat and arrange on a platter and serve with the sauce on the side.

NOTE: If you do not have a pepper mill or a mortar and pestle, you can crush the peppercorns on a cutting board or other hard surface using the bottom of a skillet.

BEARDED LADIES

Suddenly I am surrounded by goats. One offers her head for me to scratch, another nibbles at my trousers, and a third investigates my shoes, without finding anything of interest. When Lars Tyssebotn, a sturdy farmer in his late forties, lets his goats out in the morning, nothing even remotely edible is safe. The goats crowd the hillside and will not let anybody, particularly not an exotic city boy like me with funny clothes and funny smells of unknown things, pass without a thorough inspection.

Lars is a maverick, one of by Norway's few remaining goat farmers. His goats are allowed to live life as nature intended, roaming the hillsides, eating whatever they can find. Once a necessary and much-appreciated part of every farm, goats are not particularly popular anymore, and their often-tough meat and strong-tasting milk fail to compete with other meats and milk, although goat milk still has its role in the production of goat cheese.

There are two main goat cheese varieties in Norway, one a white cheese, not unlike the French *chèvres,* which is produced only to a very limited extent and considered a rarity. Far more important is brown goat cheese, *gjetost,* also known as Norwegian fudge cheese (a version of which can be found in American stores under the name of Ski Queen; see Mail-Order Sources, page 294). This brown goat cheese is the most important cheese in Norway, and for many it is a part of the daily diet, eaten with bread for breakfast or lunch.

Brown goat cheese is one of the most peculiar cheeses in the world and has no known relatives. It has a light brown color, a smooth fudgelike texture, and a mild sweet caramel flavor, with a tinge of goat. Its production is also quite different from that of other cheeses; it's made from whey, not milk, so technically it is not a cheese at all, but a fudge. But to all Norwegians, that distinction is only of academic interest; it has always been viewed and treated as a cheese.

Making cheese from whey was probably a result of poverty. The goats were cherished for their impressive survival skills and their limited demand for feed. When they were on their summer pasture, they found food in the mountains and produced plenty of milk. The rest of the year, though, they had to make do with scraps and leaves, and they hardly gave milk. But during the summer there was even more milk than needed, so the surplus had to be conserved somehow for the hard winters; making cheese from whey was a way to make sure that nothing went to waste. Throughout the eighteenth century, the sweet fudge cheese grew to be more popular than the original white goat cheese, and today the whey is considered the main asset and the milk a by-product.

Watching Lars make brown goat cheese is an interesting experience. In his small production room next to the barn, the cheese is made almost the same way it was by dairymaids a hundred years ago; the only difference is that Lars has an electric cooker with rotating arms to make production easier. The pale white whey is boiled for ten to twelve hours under constant stirring. The whey is condensed through evaporation, and after a few hours, when most of the water has evaporated, the sugars in the whey start to caramelize, and it slowly turns a light brown. Controlling the process, making sure that there is sufficient caramelization without the cheese being burned, requires skill and precision. The cooking continues until what remains is a thick brown fudge, whereupon Lars pours the cheese into molds and covers them with wax.

The brown goat cheese has an overwhelmingly sweet flavor that does not easily combine with other foods. Therefore, it is generally eaten with bread or *lefse,* the Norwegian potato cake, and only rarely used in cooking. One exception is the traditional sauce to accompany moose, reindeer, or venison, where the intense sweetness blends with the gamy flavors of the meat.

In Norway, moose and reindeer meat are much more common than venison, but the area of western Norway where Lars's farm is located is full of deer that often graze right outside his house. Lars is an ardent hunter, and he hunts with much of the same

care and respect for nature he shows with his goats. He does not want to join a shooting party because he feels chasing the animals unnecessarily will upset them, which is not good for the animals and will affect the quality of their meat. Instead, he shoots the deer on his own farm, sometimes waiting for them just outside the house. The venison with brown goat cheese sauce I had at Lars's farm was so good I feared that I would never taste anything like it again. But I have made the same dish several times in the States, and although I do not have the privilege of having walked the same field as the deer and having been nibbled at by the goat, the flavors are not all that different.

Juniper-Spiced Venison with Brown Goat Cheese Sauce

SERVES 4

THE *GJETOST* OR BROWN GOAT CHEESE IN THE RECIPE IS NOT MADE FROM MILK BUT FROM WHEY THAT IS COOKED UNTIL CARAMELIZED. IT IS ALSO KNOWN AS FUDGE CHEESE, AND A VERSION CALLED SKI QUEEN CAN BE FOUND IN MANY AMERICAN MARKETS (SEE MAIL-ORDER SOURCES, PAGE 294).

LINGONBERRY PRESERVES CAN BE FOUND IN SOME SUPERMARKETS AND IN SPECIALTY STORES (SEE MAIL-ORDER SOURCES, PAGE 294). CRANBERRIES CAN BE USED AS A SUBSTITUTE.

Four ½-pound venison fillets

8 juniper berries, crushed

1 teaspoon crushed fennel seeds

Fine sea salt and freshly ground black pepper

1 tablespoon all-purpose flour

1 cup game or beef stock

½ cup sour cream

½ to 1 ounce *gjetost* or Norwegian fudge cheese (Ski Queen), sliced

2 tablespoons unsalted butter

1 to 2 tablespoons aquavit or Mock Aquavit (page 293)

Lingonberry preserves (see headnote) or whole-berry cranberry sauce

Pat the meat dry with paper towels. Combine 6 of the juniper berries, the fennel seeds, 1 teaspoon salt, and 1 teaspoon pepper. Rub the meat with the spices and place it on a plate. Set aside at room temperature while you make the sauce.

Put the flour in a small bowl and whisk in ¼ cup of the stock; make sure there are no lumps. Pour into a small saucepan, add another ¼ cup stock, and bring to a boil, whisking constantly. When the mixture has started to thicken, stir in the remaining ½ cup stock and bring to a boil. Add the sour cream and the remaining 2 juniper berries, reduce the heat, and simmer for 2 to 3 minutes. Add the brown cheese and stir until melted and incorporated. Set the sauce aside.

Heat the butter in a cast-iron or other heavy skillet over high heat. Sear the fillets for 5 minutes, turning to brown on all sides. Transfer the meat to a plate and let rest for 4 to 5 minutes. Return the meat to the skillet and cook for 3 to 4 more minutes, until medium-rare. Let rest for 5 minutes.

Meanwhile, add the aquavit to the sauce and bring to a simmer over medium heat. Season with salt and pepper to taste.

Cut the fillets into ½-inch slices and place on four plates. Drizzle the sauce over the meat. Serve immediately, with lingonberry preserves on the side.

Lars Tyssebotn's brown goat cheese makes this dish one of my favorites.

Serve with Brussels Sprouts with Lemon and Parsley (page 234) and Potato Gratin with Parsnips and Rutabaga (page 72), or Caramelized Potatoes (page 76) and a green salad.

Simple Terrine of Game with Orange, Sage, and Pistachios

SERVES 10 AS AN APPETIZER

Baking at low temperatures, as for this recipe, can be difficult, as domestic ovens are generally inaccurate. Using a meat (or instant-read) thermometer will ensure the best results.

The terrine is great party food, and it can be made a day in advance. It also keeps well for 3 to 4 days in the refrigerator.

Serve with bread, a green salad, mustard, and port jelly or red currant jelly.

1 pound finely chopped venison (see headnote)

1 pound ground pork

2 teaspoons chopped fresh thyme

2 teaspoons chopped fresh sage

¼ teaspoon freshly grated nutmeg

2 juniper berries, crushed

1 tablespoon finely grated orange zest

⅓ cup shelled pistachios

2 teaspoons fine sea salt

¼ cup aquavit, Cognac, or other brandy

1 large egg

1 cup heavy (whipping) cream

¼ cup duck or goose fat, lard, or unsalted butter

5 slices bacon

3 bay leaves

4 orange slices

In a medium bowl, combine the venison, pork, thyme, sage, nutmeg, juniper berries, orange zest, pistachios, salt, and aquavit, mixing well. Cover and refrigerate for at least 6 hours or up to a day.

Preheat the oven to 250°F.

Add the egg, cream, and duck fat to the meat mixture and mix thoroughly. Line a 2-quart terrine mold or 9-by-5-inch loaf pan with the bacon, laying the strips across the bottom and up the sides. Add the meat mixture, then fold the ends of the bacon over the top. Arrange the bay leaves and orange slices on top. Insert a meat thermometer, if you have one, in the terrine. Bake on the lowest oven rack for approximately 1½ hours, until the temperature reaches 160°F on the meat thermometer (or an instant-read thermometer). Let cool.

Slice the terrine into ½-inch slices and serve.

10

KITCHEN OF LIGHT

CHRISTMAS: SAME PROCEDURE EVERY YEAR

The question was as inevitable as the darkness of winter. November had just laid her cold damp hands on us, and the merchants had already begun to set up their kitschy Christmas decorations. And, just as sure as there would be six weeks of pre-Christmas parties, shopping, and preparations, there would also be the ever-returning question: "So, what are you having for Christmas?" meaning, "What are you and your family eating for Christmas Eve supper?" I have always tried to dodge the subject, for I know I cannot answer to the satisfaction of the questioner.

In Norway, Christmas dinner is the most important meal of the year. It is the one time when otherwise modern people return to their roots, to what they perceive as an unchangeable tradition. This one time of year, they lay aside their balsamic vinegar, Thai curry, prefabricated pizzas, and whatever else they eat the rest of the year and cook what they grew up with, the way Mother made it. If done any other way, it would not be Christmas.

The Christmas food traditions are not uniform—there are at least six recognized Norwegian Christmas supper variations. In northern and southern Norway, cod with its liver and roe is common. To the west, *pinnekjøtt*—dried, salted, and smoked lamb ribs steamed and served with mashed rutabaga—holds its firm grip on tradition. A little farther north, in the stockfish-exporting cities of Kristiansund and Ålesund, the Portuguese-inspired *bacalao*—salted and dried cod, reconstituted and cooked with tomatoes, chiles, and pimientos—reigns. And for those traveling the wilder shores of cooking, *rakfisk*—fermented trout—and *lutefisk*—dried cod reconstituted in lye, not as dangerous as it sounds but not exactly delectable, either—are powerful reminders of a time when unhinged creativity was the only way to ensure survival through hard times. The most popular and geographically neutral dish, however, is *ribbe*—rib roast of pork with a crisp crackling.

People are attached to their Christmas tradition in much the same way they are attached to an old relative they see only once a year—he may not be kind or interesting, but he is family, after all, and that is what matters most. I have met people who hate *lutefisk* or *ribbe* and would never think of eating it at any other time of year but who would rather starve than go without it on Christmas Eve.

The question about what you are eating for Christmas supper is of enormous importance. The answer says something about where you are from and what kind of Norwegian-ness you identify with. My answer, although amiable from a purely gastronomical point of view, is hardly ever accepted: "I eat different things each year," I tell people, and I am almost always met with stunned silence, followed by an endless inquisition: How is it possible? does it not feel meaningless? and, most of all, how did it come to be that way? To some it sounds like a liberating lack of traditions, to others like pure nihilism, a mockery, rather like pouring solvent into the glue of shared nationhood.

There are good reasons why it has come to be this way: My parents divorced when I was a young child, and I spent most Christmases with my mother. Because we were only two, we often spent Christmas Eve with friends and relatives, so we ate whatever they ate. Sometimes the food was good, occasionally it was catastrophic, but most of the time it was plain but enjoyable. And it was hardly ever the same two years in a row. As I grew older and my mother and I started to have Christmas by ourselves, we did not have a fixed tradition to build upon, so we continued our drift, this time not out of necessity, but out of curiosity and hunger and what had unintentionally become our very own tradition. Over the years, my Christmas table has seen both unusual exotic dishes and conventional Christmas fare, but the times I have been most happy have been when I have been able to take something well used and traditional and make it into something that tastes fresh and new.

After all the questions are answered, my tradition, or lack thereof, is generally accepted with overbearing amusement. Sometimes it is even found to have its advantages, especially when negotiating a joint Christmas Eve celebration. And when discussing how to get the perfect crackling on the *ribbe,*

I can announce that, in order to ensure a sufficient variation, I have tried more than a few different ways to get the crackling more crackling and the meat more juicy, and I can assure them that the traditional way to cook the roast— by covering it with foil and letting it steam before broiling it until crackling—is indeed the best. And when that is done, I will provoke either anger or interest when mentioning that the roast will taste even better, juicier, and more Christmasy if spiked with cloves, and somewhat lighter if marinated in orange juice.

Cooking different foods every year allows me to investigate different Christmas foods, to combine traditional food with innovation, and, of course, to make Christmas the way my mother did when I was growing up.

Pork Rib Roast with Cloves

SERVES 6

Ribbe, as the traditional Christmas supper is called in Norwegian, has a special position in Norway, something almost as sacred as the Thanksgiving turkey in America. Almost everyone I know eats pork rib roast, and for them a Christmas without it would be unthinkable.

The measure of success is how well the crackling turns out. There is a fine balance between getting the fat hot enough for it to start crackling, but not so hot that it burns. I have found that a convection oven is the best for this purpose (a normal oven is also fine, but it is not so easy to get an even result). If you cannot find a pork rib roast with fat and rind, you will miss out on the crackling, but the dish is still very good.

I always cook onions and potatoes in the roasting pan. A more traditional way would be to serve Mashed Rutabaga (page 198). Some strong mustard is also good with the fatty meat. The roast ideally should be salted and marinated in orange juice for 1 to 2 days before cooking, to make the meat more tender and flavorful.

One 4-pound pork rib roast, with rind and fat, bones cut at 3-inch intervals (have the butcher do this)

1 tablespoon fine sea salt

2 teaspoons freshly ground black pepper

3 oranges

2 tablespoons chopped fresh sage

A handful of whole cloves

2 pounds russet potatoes, quartered

1 pound onions, quartered

Place the meat skin side up on a cutting board. With a sharp heavy knife, cut through the rind and fat to make a crosshatch pattern with 1-inch squares. With a thin sharp knife, make a small slit in each square. (This is where you will insert the cloves; you could insert them now, but I have found that all the handling is likely to break off most of the nice-looking tops of the cloves.) Rub the meat with the salt and pepper.

Place the meat in a baking dish. Cut 1 orange in half and squeeze the juice over the meat. Slice another orange and place the slices under and over the meat. Cover and refrigerate for 1 to 2 days, turning three or four times.

Preheat the oven to 400°F.

Discard the orange and place the meat fat side down in a roasting pan. Insert the sage between the cut ribs. Turn the meat skin side up. Cut the remaining orange in half and squeeze the juice over the meat. Cut the orange halves into smaller pieces and place them under the meat. Insert a clove in each of the slits in the fat.

Cover the roast with foil. Place the roasting pan in the middle of the oven and roast for 45 minutes. Remove from the oven and reduce the temperature to 350°F. Remove the foil. Remove the meat from the pan and add potatoes and onions to the pan, making a foundation for the meat. Return the meat to the pan and place in the oven, this time setting it in the lower third of the oven; roast for about 1 hour.

Move the pan to the middle of the oven. Increase the heat to 400° to 425°F and roast for about 20 minutes longer under frequent surveillance to produce a good crackling. If you have a top oven broiler, you could use it, but be very careful that you don't burn the roast. It is difficult to give the exact time for the crackling process, since that depends on the intensity of heat in your oven. If there is no sign of crackling after 10 minutes, gradually turn the heat up to 450°F. The crackling will be superb if it looks as if the rind is boiling and the fatty squares have started to separate. Remove and allow to cool slightly.

Cut the meat into 2-rib sections and place on serving plates. The meat looks nice served with the cloves, but be advised that they should be removed before eating, as they are still quite strong-tasting.

Breast of Goose with Apples, Prunes, and Port Reduction

SERVES 4

The most touching story by the Danish fairy-tale writer Hans Christian Andersen is, no doubt, the story of the Little Match Stick Girl, about a poor girl who freezes to death in the cold on Christmas Eve. The last thing she does is warm herself on her unsold matches while smelling the goose cooking in a nearby house.

With the danger of being somewhat inappropriate, this is the traditional Danish way of serving goose—almost exactly the same dish as the one the Little Match Stick Girl never got to taste. I have modernized it a bit, mainly by adding a few drops of balsamic vinegar.

Two 16- to 20-ounce boneless goose breasts, skin on (see Note)

Fine sea salt and freshly ground black pepper

3 tablespoons balsamic vinegar

2 garlic cloves, minced

3 tablespoons chopped fresh sage

3 tablespoons unsalted butter

3 tablespoons chopped shallots

1/2 cup Goose or Duck Stock (page 18) or chicken stock

1/2 cup ruby port

2 bay leaves

5 black peppercorns

1/2 teaspoon coriander seeds

3 tablespoons sugar

2 sweet apples, such as Golden Delicious, peeled (optional), cored, and cut into 1-inch dice

1/4 pound (about 1 cup) prunes, pitted and halved

Preheat the oven to 300°F.

With a sharp knife, make a crisscross pattern in the fatty skin of the goose breasts. Season liberally with salt and pepper. Heat a cast-iron or other heavy skillet over high heat. Add the goose breasts skin side down, reduce the heat to medium-high, and cook for 5 to 6 minutes, until the skin is crispy. Flip and cook for 2 minutes on the other side. Remove from the heat.

Place the goose breasts skin side up in a baking dish. Drizzle with 1 tablespoon of the balsamic vinegar, scatter half the minced garlic and 1 tablespoon of the sage over them. and season with salt. Bake for 25 to 30 minutes, until the center of the meat reaches 145°F on an instant-read thermometer. Transfer to a cutting board and let rest, uncovered, for at least 15 minutes. Set the baking dish aside.

Meanwhile, in a small saucepan, heat 2 teaspoons of the butter over medium heat. Sauté the shallots and the remaining garlic for 3 to 4 minutes. Add the stock, 6 tablespoons of the port, 1 tablespoon of the balsamic vinegar, 1 tablespoon of the sage, the bay leaves, peppercorns, and coriander seeds. If there are any cooking juices from the goose left in the baking dish, add them to the pan. Reduce over medium heat until about 1/4 cup is left. Strain the sauce and return it to the pan. Set aside.

In a small nonstick skillet, heat the sugar over medium heat until it melts and becomes a light brown caramel. Add the remaining 1 tablespoon balsamic vinegar and 2 tablespoons port. Cook for 2 to 3 minutes until you have a thick syrup, then add the apples and prunes and cook for 3 to 4 minutes. Add the remaining 1 tablespoon sage and salt to taste.

Meanwhile, just before serving, return the port reduction a boil and stir in the rest of the butter; do not let boil.

Slice the goose breasts. Place on four individual plates, along with the apples and prunes. Pour the port reduction over the goose and serve immediately.

NOTE: If the goose breasts are skinned, cook them in 3 tablespoons goose fat or butter.

Prune-Stuffed Pork Meatballs with Beet Salad

SERVES 4

I prefer to serve the meatballs on their own, rather than with other meats, accompanied by Caramelized Potatoes (page 76) and a green salad or Savoy Cabbage with Dill Butter and Bacon (page 237) without the bacon.

2½ pounds finely ground pork (about 30 percent fat)

¼ cup potato starch or all-purpose flour

½ teaspoon freshly grated nutmeg

½ teaspoon ground ginger

2 teaspoons fine sea salt

2 cups whole milk

10 prunes, pitted and chopped

1 sweet apple, such as Golden Delicious, peeled, cored, and chopped

2 teaspoons chopped caraway seeds, crushed

1 to 2 teaspoons curry powder

½ cup water

2 to 3 tablespoons unsalted butter

Beet Salad (recipe follows)

Combine the ground pork, potato starch, nutmeg, ginger, salt, and milk in a large bowl and mix well with your hands until you have a smooth, thick, sticky mixture.

In a small saucepan, combine the prunes, apple, caraway seeds, curry powder, and ½ cup water. Bring to a boil over medium-low heat. Reduce the heat to low and boil gently until all the water has evaporated and you have a thick paste. Remove from the heat and let cool off for a few minutes, until nicely warm.

Divide the pork mixture into 20 more or less equal pieces. Flatten one piece at a time with the back of a spoon until it is approximately 2 inches in diameter. Place 1 teaspoon of the prune mixture in the middle of the pork mixture and fold the pork mixture up around it to make a round ball.

Heat the butter in a large nonstick skillet over medium heat. Add only as many meatballs as will fit in the skillet without crowding it and cook, turning frequently, for 8 to 10 minutes, until the meatballs are cooked through. Add more butter if needed.

Transfer the meatballs to a serving platter or bowl and cook the remaining meatballs. Serve with the Beet Salad.

Beet Salad

1 cup coarsely chopped
pickled beets

¼ cup chopped dill pickles
(pickled gherkins)

½ green apple, such as
Granny Smith, peeled, cored,
and chopped

1 tablespoon grated horseradish

3 tablespoons sour cream,
or more to taste

Apple cider vinegar to taste

Combine the beets, pickles, apple, horseradish,
and sour cream in a medium bowl, mixing well.
Add apple cider vinegar to taste, which depends
on how sour the pickles are. I seldom use more
than 1 to 2 teaspoons.

The Beet Salad is not really a salad,
but rather a sweet-and-sour condiment.

Aquavit-Flambéed Pork Loin Chops with Apple and Onion Compote

SERVES 4

Serve with Caramelized Potatoes
(page 76), Red Cabbage Compote
(page 214), and Baked Fennel
(page 236).

**Four ½-pound pork chops,
1 inch thick**

**⅓ cup aquavit, Mock Aquavit,
(page 293), or brandy**

1 garlic clove, finely chopped

½ teaspoon fennel seeds

½ teaspoon caraway seeds

½ teaspoon cumin seeds

3 tablespoons unsalted butter

3 onions, chopped

**4 sweet apples, such as Golden
Delicious, peeled (optional),
cored, and diced**

**Fine sea salt and freshly ground
black pepper**

2 tablespoons vegetable oil

Place the chops in a bowl. Add 3 tablespoons of
the aquavit, the garlic, and half of each of the fennel
seeds, caraway seeds, and cumin seeds. Cover
and refrigerate for 12 to 24 hours, turning once.

To make the compote, heat 1 tablespoon of the
butter in a large saucepan over medium-high
heat. Cook the onions for 5 minutes, or until they
have browned nicely. Add the apples and cook
for 10 minutes, until tender but still firm inside.

Remove the chops from the marinade (reserve the
marinade) and pat dry with paper towels. Season
with salt and pepper and the remaining fennel seeds,
caraway seeds, and cumin seeds. Heat the vegetable
oil in a large skillet over high heat. Sear the steaks
over high heat for 2 minutes on each side. Reduce
the heat and cook for 2 minutes longer on each
side. Combine the marinade and the rest of the
aquavit, add to the skillet, and carefully set it alight.
(The flame can be quite high at the start.) Allow
the flame to die out.

Transfer the pork to a serving platter with the
apple and onion compote. Allow the marinade to
cook gently for an additional 20 seconds, then
stir in the remaining 2 tablespoons butter and pour
over the chops.

RUTABAGA: WHAT ALL NORWEGIANS ARE THINKING ABOUT

According to the Norwegian anthropologist Runar Døving, rutabaga is what all Norwegians are thinking of but do not dare to talk about. This somewhat puzzling assertion is made on the basis of some astounding statistics and Døving's fieldwork and personal experiences.

But if we love the rutabaga, why don't we talk about it? In his influential essay *"Brassica Napus"* (the Latin name for rutabaga), Døving found that people have a strong urge to talk about it, to discuss recipes, cooking times, preferences (waxed or unwaxed), and its somewhat unfortunate looks, but there is no tradition of talking about it. You can discuss the way you like your meat cooked or the fine nuances of cooking the traditional Christmas rib roast. But the rutabaga's lack of prestige prevents us from talking about it, making it "what everybody is thinking about but no one knows how to talk about."

While they barely utter the word, Norwegians insist on a different kind of rutabaga than the other remaining rutabaga nation, Sweden. The Norwegian rutabaga has orange-yellow flesh, while the Swedish

rutabaga is white. In each country, the other sort would be categorized as an inferior item.

Luckily, there are some signs that the rutabaga is coming back to a position of prominence, perhaps even greater than before. After all, it has, against all odds, managed to keep its position both on the weekday dinner table and at many traditional feasts. At the same time, a few innovative chefs are pulling the modest vegetable out from the dark, dressing it up like a king, and serving it in ways one would never have thought possible—with truffles, infused with vanilla, or as part of a luxurious potato gratin. And who knows, one day we might be able to start talking about it, too.

Mashed Rutabaga

SERVES 6 AS A SIDE DISH

1/2 cup salt

2 pounds rutabaga, peeled and cut into 1 1/2-inch cubes

1/2 pound carrots, peeled and cut into 1 1/2-inch pieces

1/2 pound potatoes, peeled and cut into 1 1/2-inch cubes

1 to 2 tablespoons unsalted butter

1/4 teaspoon freshly grated nutmeg

Fine sea salt and freshly ground black pepper

In a large pot, combine the salt and 3 quarts water and bring to a boil over high heat. Add the rutabaga, carrots, and potatoes and cook over medium heat for 25 to 35 minutes, or until the rutabaga is soft. Drain well.

Mash with a potato masher or blend in a food processor until smooth. Add the butter. Season with the nutmeg and salt and pepper to taste.

Home-Churned Butter

MAKES APPROXIMATELY 2½ CUPS

3 cups sour cream

1 cup heavy (whipping) cream

Fine sea salt

Place the sour cream and cream in a blender and blend on high speed for 15 to 20 minutes, until the cream separates into yellow butter lumps and white buttermilk. Strain and reserve the buttermilk for other purposes.

With your hands, squeeze out as much of the remaining buttermilk as you can before the heat of your hands starts melting the butter. Place the butter in a large bowl of cold water and continue squeezing gently for 2 minutes, until the water is white. Transfer to a small bowl and add salt to taste. Cover and refrigerate. Remove from the refrigerator 20 minutes before serving.

The most appreciated butter is called Kvitseid butter and is made from the milk of cows grazing on summer mountain pastures. It contains more salt and is made from slightly soured cream, giving it an almost cheeselike complexity.

It is not often I take the time to make my own butter, but when I do, often at Christmas, the difference between it and commercial butter is remarkable. I make my own butter from sour cream, and the result is very similar to the traditional Kvitseid butter. (The slightly sour buttermilk that is left is excellent in bread dough or Christmas morning pancake batter.)

The butter will keep for 1 week, refrigerated; it can be frozen for up to 2 months.

11

THE HIGH LIFE

Stopping on a small hilltop to rest, I suddenly got the feeling that I had been at this same place before. I could swear that the bare rocks I was sitting on had exactly the same pattern as the ones I had stopped by three days (and half a dozen blisters) ago. The landscape also looked familiar. From where I was sitting, I could see green moors, dotted with white bog cotton and long stretches of red heather, framed by a mountain ridge that looked like a row of falling dominos. A deep, calm tiredness penetrated my body. Through my drooping eyelids I could see a small group of grouse landing near some juniper bushes less than two hundred feet from me. I leaned back and fell asleep in the warm, soft light of the August sun.

In the wilderness of the Norwegian highlands, life is different. Time does not stand still, but it does move with a different pace from the rest of the world. I had walked for nearly three days and met only two other people. Walking westward, I had seen the landscape slowly change, snow-capped mountains appearing and disappearing in the distance to the north and south of me, sometimes pointed and dramatic, sometimes just soft curves of gray without anything to fix one's eye on. At times, the landscape seemed oddly familiar, like a *déjà vu,* in which the landscape of my mind was merging with the physical landscape.

I was in my own company but not lonely. On the first, windy night, I had tented in a level between two small hilltops, clearly a popular spot. The grass bore marks that a deer or some other wild animal had slept there before me. In the morning, I awoke to find that a local fox had marked his territorial demands, and displeasure with my company, just outside the tent. The second night, I had camped in one of the old unmanned log cabins that have been set up to accommodate travelers. I shared the small cabin with a hunter and his dog. In the evening we ate supper together. When I woke the next morning, he had already departed, leaving me a grouse from his rich catch. It was still in its plumage, and looked almost alive, as if it were just resting on the table.

Here on the hilltop, the noisy flight of grouse woke me from my slumber. While I had slept, the sun had crept considerably lower on the horizon. I decided not to walk any farther that day and set up camp for the night while it was still light. Summer fades quickly in late August; the days were getting shorter and there was a cool current in the air, signaling that autumn was right around the corner.

I set up my tent, plucked the grouse, and went over to the juniper bushes where the flock of grouse had been feasting. Juniper is a favorite of grouse, and nearly all the ripe berries had been picked by the hungry visitors. Only the green unripe berries of next year were left, but after a careful search of the lowest sprigs I managed to find a small handful of ripe violet fruit that the grouse had not had time to harvest before their departure.

I cooked the grouse on my old camp stove, using nothing but butter, salt and pepper, and the juniper berries. It certainly shouldn't have been the best grouse I had ever eaten: When cooked right, grouse can be wonderfully tender and juicy; this one, however, was definitely tough and more than a little dry. Juniper berries can be overpowering, and my berries were far too much; I should have used only half, perhaps a third of what I did. And, to properly enjoy grouse, with its strong yet sophisticated flavor, one should serve it with fine wine and some hearty vegetables such as Brussels sprouts or rutabaga; I had only stale bread, marsh water, and a little cheap whiskey.

But somehow it was the best grouse I had ever tasted. There and then on that hilltop overlooking nothing but the soft green, white, and red landscape, it was perfect. After I had sopped up the last cooking juices from the pan, and finished the last drop of whiskey, I sat back and watched the sun set. And for a very long while I thought of nothing.

Breast of Grouse with Mushrooms and Pears

SERVES 2 AS A MAIN COURSE, 4 AS AN APPETIZER

Grouse has delicious but very lean meat, and if you overcook it, it becomes very tough. The best way to prevent this is to cook the grouse breast on the bone, which helps keep the meat juicy. Use an instant-read thermometer for the best result.

You need to get whole grouse in order to make the delicious stock-based sauce. If you would like to use more of the bird, you could cook the legs in duck fat for 2 hours at 200°F to make delicious grouse confit.

Serve with Panfried Potatoes with Bay Leaves, Pancetta, and Mushrooms (page 73).

2 grouse (see headnote)

4 juniper berries, crushed

Fine sea salt and freshly ground black pepper

4 tablespoons unsalted butter

3 tablespoons chopped shallots

2 garlic cloves, chopped

4 cups boiling water

1 bay leaf

5 black peppercorns

1/3 cup finely chopped celeriac

1/3 cup finely chopped carrot

1/4 cup olive oil

2 medium pears, such as Anjou, quartered

1 tablespoon chopped fresh rosemary

1/2 pound wild mushrooms, trimmed, cleaned, and cut into 1 1/2-inch pieces

2 teaspoons chopped fresh chives

1 teaspoon Dijon mustard

1 to 2 teaspoons red currant jelly or preserves

With a sharp knife, cut off the whole breast section of each bird. Cut the legs, thighs, and carcasses into smaller pieces. Season the breasts with the juniper and salt and pepper and set aside at room temperature for 45 minutes.

To make the sauce, heat 1 tablespoon of the butter in a small pot over medium heat until it bubbles energetically. Sauté 2 tablespoons of shallots and half the garlic for 3 to 4 minutes. Add the chopped pieces of grouse and sauté for 3 minutes. Add the boiling water, bay leaf, peppercorns, celeriac, and carrot, bring to a boil, and with a spoon, skim off the foam that has gathered on the surface. Reduce the heat and simmer for 20 minutes. Strain into a small saucepan and reduce to 1/3 cup. Remove from the heat and set aside.

Preheat the oven to 300°F.

In an ovenproof skillet, heat 2 tablespoons of the butter over medium-high heat. Add the grouse breasts skin side down and cook for 6 minutes, turning every now and then. Transfer the pan to the middle of the oven and cook for 12 to 15 minutes (8 to 10 minutes if deboned), until the interior temperature reaches 140°F on an instant-read thermometer. Transfer to a cutting board and let rest for 15 minutes.

While the grouse are resting, heat 1 tablespoon of the olive oil in a wide skillet over medium-high heat. Add the pears and rosemary and cook, stirring occasionally, for 4 minutes. Transfer to a bowl and set aside, covered to keep warm.

Heat the remaining 3 tablespoons olive oil in the same skillet, over medium heat. Add the mushrooms and the remaining shallots and garlic and cook for 5 to 6 minutes, until the mushrooms are tender. Season liberally with salt and pepper, and sprinkle with the chives before serving.

Just before serving, bring the reduced stock to a boil. Stir in the mustard, red currant jelly, and the remaining 1 tablespoon butter. Season with salt to taste.

Cut the breasts from the bone, slice them, and place them on warm plates. Add the pears and mushrooms, pour the sauce over the grouse breasts, and serve.

Roast Dill-Scented Chicken with Leeks and Potatoes

SERVES 4 TO 6

Dill is one of Scandinavia's favorite herbs, one that grows willingly in the cool Nordic climate. Historically, it has been important in traditional herbal medicine; dill water was used to soothe children. In fact, the name *dill* is of Nordic origin, *dilla* meaning "to lull" in Old Norse.

When I made this dish on *New Scandinavian Cooking,* we were on a farm in Lom, in the highlands, a region often referred to as the Provence of Norway. The dill grown on the farm was so good that I ate it on or with everything I put in my mouth.

Serve with Asparagus Sautéed in Butter and Mustard (page 228) or Green Pea Puree with Asparagus and Scallions (page 227).

One 4-pound free-range chicken

Fine sea salt and freshly ground black pepper

6 tablespoons unsalted butter, at room temperature

1/2 cup chopped dill, plus 1 large bunch fresh dill

1 lemon, quartered

5 to 6 medium leeks, white and light green parts only, thoroughly washed and cut into 2-inch pieces

1 1/2 pounds russet potatoes, cut into 1-inch slices

8 garlic cloves, unpeeled

3 cups chicken stock

Fresh dill for garnish

Lemon wedges and grated lemon zest for garnish

Preheat the oven to 425°F.

Rub the chicken with salt and pepper. In a small bowl, combine the butter and chopped dill. Rub the chicken with about 2 tablespoons of the dill butter. Carefully lift up the skin from the chicken breasts at the cavity, using your fingers or a blunt knife to loosen the skin; be careful not to tear it. Insert about 1 tablespoon of the dill butter under the breast skin and make sure that the skin covers the meat afterward. Refrigerate the remaining butter. Fill the cavity of the chicken with the lemon quarters and the bunch of dill.

Place the chicken breast side up on a V-shaped rack in a roasting pan. Place the roasting pan on the middle oven rack and cook the chicken for 25 minutes.

Remove the chicken from the oven and rub with about 1 tablespoon of the dill butter, holding the butter in your fingers. When most of the butter has melted and you are at risk of burning your fingers, place the remaining lump on the breast of the chicken.

Remove the roasting pan from the oven. Fill the pan with the leeks, potatoes, and garlic and add the chicken stock. Turn the chicken breast side down and place it in the roasting pan. Reduce the oven temperature to 350°F. Return the roasting pan to the oven and roast for 50 to 60 more minutes, or until the chicken is cooked through. Test for doneness by piercing it with a sharp knife at the thickest part of the thigh; the juices should run clear. (If there is any trace of pink in the juices, return the chicken to the oven.) Transfer the chicken to a carving board and let it rest, uncovered, for 15 minutes.

Check the potatoes for doneness. If they are still firm, increase the oven temperature to 400°F and continue baking until the potatoes are nice and tender. Squeeze the garlic out of their skins. Leave the roasting pan in the oven with the heat turned off.

Transfer the potatoes, leeks, and garlic to a serving platter. Carve the chicken at the table (discard the lemon and dill inside the cavity).

Garnish with dill and lemon wedges and sprinkle lemon zest on top.

Chicken with Saffron and Cinnamon

SERVES 4

Chicken is popular in Scandinavia, but today preparations do not differ much from those found in other northern European and American cuisines. If we go back in time, however, we find some unique spicy chicken dishes.

This recipe is taken from a medieval cookbook discovered in Iceland, and probably dates back to the fourteenth century. The book is really nothing more than a manuscript with helpful hints and very few directions, and I have adapted the recipe considerably for modern cooking methods.

The inclusion of saffron and cinnamon indicates that this was food for the wealthy—and is a reminder of how international the Scandinavian elite was in its orientation. Since the easiest way to travel was by sea, it was often easier to travel between remote ports in different countries than to go inland.

Serve with Mashed Rutabaga (page 198) and Green Beans and Peas with Celeriac and Mango (page 230).

One 4-pound free-range chicken, cut into 8 pieces

2 garlic cloves, minced

Pinch of saffron threads

1 teaspoon ground cinnamon

1 teaspoon fine sea salt

2 teaspoons all-purpose flour

2 tablespoons red wine vinegar

2 tablespoons olive oil

1/2 cup white wine, preferably semi-dry

2 chicken livers, finely chopped, or 1/2 chicken bouillon cube

Place the chicken pieces in one layer in a baking dish. In a small bowl, combine the garlic, saffron, cinnamon, salt, flour, vinegar, and olive oil, stirring until smooth. Rub the chicken all over with the spice mixture. Cover and let marinate for 45 minutes at room temperature, or up to 1 day in the refrigerator.

Preheat the oven to 400°F.

Bake the chicken pieces skin side up for 30 minutes.

Add the wine and chicken livers (or bouillon cube) to the pan. Bake for 20 to 30 more minutes (stirring once or twice if using a bouillon cube), or until the juices run clear—not pink—when the chicken is pierced in the thickest part with the tip of a sharp knife. Serve with bread to sop up the cooking juices.

Sugar-and-Spice-Crusted Squab Breast

SERVES 2

FOR THIS RECIPE, PARTRIDGE OR GROUSE, OR DUCK BREASTS THAT HAVE BEEN TRIMMED OF FAT, CAN BE SUBSTITUTED FOR THE SQUAB BREAST. I HAVE EVEN MADE THIS WITH CHICKEN COOKED IN GOOSE FAT, THOUGH IT LACKS THE GAMY QUALITIES THAT MAKE THE DISH REALLY INTERESTING.

1 tablespoon beef marrow or unsalted butter

1/2 teaspoon finely grated orange zest

2 teaspoons ground cumin, preferably freshly ground

1 teaspoon ground anise, preferably freshly ground

2 teaspoons freshly ground black pepper

1 teaspoon fine sea salt

1 tablespoon unsalted butter

4 squab breasts (see Mail-Order Sources, page 294)

2 tablespoons brown sugar

1/2 garlic clove, crushed

Preheat the oven to 400°F.

In a small bowl, combine the marrow with half the orange zest, cumin, anise, and pepper and all the salt. Rub the squab breasts with the mixture. Let stand at room temperature for 45 minutes.

Heat the butter in a large skillet over medium heat until golden brown. Sear the squab breasts for 2 minutes on both sides.

Transfer the squab to a baking dish and bake for 5 minutes. Transfer to a plate and let rest for 5 minutes. Reserve the cooking juices in the pan.

Preheat the broiler.

On a small plate, mix the brown sugar with the remaining orange zest, cumin, anise, and pepper and the garlic. Roll the squab breasts in the sugar mixture and place them on a flat baking rack. Place the rack under the broiler and the baking dish underneath. Broil for 2 minutes, or until the sugar has melted. Transfer the squab to plates and let rest for 3 to 4 minutes before serving.

Serve the squab with the cooking juices.

In 1998, Norwegian chef Terje Ness won the unofficial world championship in cooking, the Bocuse d'Or, by making one stunning creation with pollock and scallops and one with squab.

I tasted the menu several times as he was preparing for the competition, and his different experiments with squab were all excellent, from luxurious truffled versions with lots of foie gras to the more traditional game preparations. He finally decided on a bold and spicy version.

Re-creating the dish takes a world champion, but Terje taught me how to make a simplified version that can easily be made at home. It contains all the flavors of the winning dish.

Serve with Caramelized Potatoes (page 76) and Brussels Sprouts with Lemon and Parsley (page 234) or Green Pea Puree with Asparagus and Scallions (page 227).

L▸R Sugar-and-Spice-Crusted Squab Breast, page 211. Squab with Pistachios and Chanterelle Potatoes.

Squab with Pistachios and Chanterelle Potatoes

SERVES 2

SQUAB HAS VERY FINE, MILDLY FLAVORED GAMY MEAT, BUT THIS RECIPE ALSO WORKS WELL WITH THE MORE STRONGLY FLAVORED GROUSE OR THE MILDER PARTRIDGE, AS WELL AS WITH PHEASANT.

4 small squab breasts or two 8-ounce pheasant or partridge breasts (see Mail-Order Sources, page 294)

1 pound russet potatoes, thinly sliced

2 ounces chanterelles, trimmed, cleaned, and thinly sliced

1 large garlic clove, thinly sliced

Fine sea salt and freshly ground black pepper

2 tablespoons plus 2 teaspoons unsalted butter

1/2 teaspoon caraway seeds

2 tablespoons finely chopped pistachios

1 teaspoon toasted sesame oil

Preheat the oven to 350°F.

Let the squab breasts stand at room temperature for 45 minutes before cooking. Meanwhile, layer the potato slices in a small baking dish, placing the chanterelles and garlic in between the layers. Season with salt and pepper. Dot with 2 tablespoons of the butter. Bake for 45 minutes.

In a medium skillet, heat the remaining 2 teaspoons butter over medium-high heat. Sear the squab breasts for 2 minutes on each side, or until golden brown. (If using pheasant, cook for 4 minutes on each side, until golden brown.) Transfer to a plate and let stand for 2 to 3 minutes, until cool enough to handle.

Rub the squab breasts with salt and pepper, the caraway, pistachios, and sesame oil. Place on top of the potatoes and cook for 7 to 9 minutes (slightly longer for pheasant), until the interior temperature reaches 140°F on an instant-read thermometer.

Let rest for 5 to 7 minutes before serving.

Glazed Duck with Red Cabbage Compote and Orange Sauce

SERVES 4

Serve with Panfried Potatoes with Bay Leaves, Pancetta, and Mushrooms (page 73).

1½ pounds red cabbage, finely shredded

¼ cup red currant jelly

1½ cups red wine

1½ cups plus 3 tablespoons water

2 tablespoons red wine vinegar, or more to taste

6 tablespoons sugar

5 tablespoons unsalted butter, or less as needed

2 whole cloves

Fine sea salt and freshly ground black pepper

Two 16- to 20-ounce boneless duck breasts, skin on (see Note)

2 tablespoons honey

1 tablespoon plus 1 teaspoon chopped fresh thyme

1½ cups fresh orange juice

1 bay leaf

2 teaspoons fresh lemon juice (optional)

1 teaspoon grated orange zest for garnish

To make the cabbage compote, combine the cabbage, currant jelly, red wine, 1½ cups water, the vinegar, 4 tablespoons of the sugar, 2 tablespoons of the butter, and the cloves in a small pot. Bring to a boil over medium heat, cover, reduce the heat, and simmer gently for 45 minutes. Remove the lid and cook for another 20 minutes, until thick and syrupy. Make sure the compote does not boil dry; add more water if necessary. Season with salt and pepper, and add more vinegar to taste. Remove from the heat and set aside.

Preheat the oven to 350°F.

With a sharp knife, score a crisscross pattern in the skin of the duck breasts. Season liberally with salt and pepper. Heat a cast-iron or other heavy skillet over medium-high heat. Add the duck breasts skin side down and cook for 5 to 6 minutes, until the skin is crispy. Turn and cook for 2 minutes on the other side.

Transfer the breasts to a baking dish. Rub them with the honey and 1 tablespoon of the thyme. Season again with salt and pepper. Bake skin side up on the middle oven rack for 15 minutes, or until the interior temperature reaches 140°F on an instant-read thermometer. Transfer the duck to a cutting board and let it rest for at least 15 minutes. Set the baking dish aside.

Meanwhile, in a small nonstick pot, cook the remaining 2 tablespoons sugar and the remaining

3 tablespoons water until the sugar dissolves and becomes a light caramel. Add the orange juice, bay leaf, the remaining 1 teaspoon thyme, and any cooking juices from the duck, bring to a boil, and reduce to ⅓ cup. Strain into a small saucepan and discard the solids. Add lemon juice to taste. Just before serving, stir in the remaining 3 tablespoons butter (if there was a lot of duck fat in the cooking juices, use less butter).

Reheat the cabbage compote, then place in a serving bowl. Carve the duck into thin slices and arrange on a serving platter. Pour the sauce over the duck and garnish with the orange zest. Serve immediately.

NOTE: If the duck breasts are skinned, cook them in 2 tablespoons duck fat or butter.

12

A SECRET PLACE

Everybody has a secret place, a place that no one else knows of. My secret place is just a twenty-minute train ride and then a fifteen-minute walk from my apartment in the center of Oslo. It is beautiful and quiet—a small clearing in the woods where, from a distance, you can see the cityscape and observe the activity on the Oslo fjord—but these qualities are only the added value. What attracts me to the place, and what makes me guard the secret of its whereabouts so carefully, are the mushrooms. In a small stretch less than a hundred feet long on the west side of the clearing, hidden in between blueberry bushes, mosses, and slowly decaying leaves, there is an abundance of chanterelles. Together with the newly fallen bright yellow birch leaves, they light up the dark ground like gold ore.

There is a quiet drama and competitiveness in foraging for the golden chanterelles (like the Klondike, but without the wolves and the gangrene and everything that made the Klondike so unpleasant). From early August

to mid-October, Norwegians of all ages venture into the forest to pick chanterelles.

Nowhere is the national obsession for mushrooming more evident than in Oslo. On Sundays, the subways out of town are full of people with wicker baskets and knives, and the air is thick with quiet anticipation. While Norwegians are normally quite sociable, there is something reserved about everybody as we head out to mushroom. People guard their favorite places jealously and will happily take long detours to make sure they are not being followed. My place is well hidden, way off the beaten path, but still I take all the necessary precautions to keep it a secret.

When I have safely made it to the clearing, the mushrooming itself is easy. Finding the mushrooms takes a trained eye and not much more. Most of the chanterelles are growing in the shadows amid the moss, and their color is nearly indistinguishable from that of the golden birch leaves. If you think all that shimmers is gold, you will have to turn many leaves before you find enough mushrooms for supper. But once your eye has adjusted to spotting the difference, the rest is easy. Chanterelles always grow in small, circular formations, and when you have spotted one mushroom, you can be sure to find many more close by. During the slow process of poking in the moss and looking underneath fallen branches, I almost fall into a trance, and before I know it, an hour or more has passed.

On the subway back to town, the mood has changed dramatically. People show off their harvest and the true mushroom connoisseurs tell you to look for rare fungi as well, displaying some strange-looking specimens that they claim to be as good as, or better than, the chanterelles, hedgehog mushrooms, and porcini of everyman. But they will not tell you where to look for them.

Minutes after the subway starts moving away from Sognsvann station, we are back in the city center. There is a special look to the mushroomers who are reentering town, the blissful expression of people carrying a treasure—and guarding a secret.

I always feel great when I return from these small expeditions, and cooking the mushrooms fills me with a hunter's pride. Like almost all true delicacies, chanterelles demand restraint more than technical ability from the cook. Frying them in butter and seasoning only with salt, pepper, and parsley is enough to transport you out of this world.

Wild Mushroom Ragout

SERVES 4 TO 6

WILD MUSHROOMS OFTEN HAVE SOIL ON THEM, BUT THEY SHOULD BE CLEANED WITHOUT WATER, PREFERABLY WITH A DAMP CLOTH OR SOFT BRUSH. NEWLY PICKED MUSHROOMS CONTAIN A LOT OF WATER. IF YOU ARE USING OLDER MUSHROOMS, YOU MAY NEED MORE BUTTER. YOU COULD ALSO ADD A FEW TABLESPOONS OF WATER.

THIS IS A SIMPLE DISH THAT GOES WELL WITH ALMOST EVERYTHING: FRIED FISH, POULTRY, MEAT, AND GAME.

2 tablespoons unsalted butter

2 tablespoons finely chopped shallots

1 pound mixed wild mushrooms, such as chanterelles, porcini, boletus, and hedgehog, trimmed, cleaned, and cut into $\frac{1}{3}$-inch slices no more than 2 inches long

2 teaspoons red wine vinegar

Fine sea salt and freshly ground black pepper

2 tablespoons chopped fresh parsley

In a large deep sauté pan, heat the butter over medium-high heat. Sauté the shallots for 1 to 2 minutes. Add the mushrooms and cook for 5 to 7 minutes, stirring a couple of times. Add the vinegar and cook for 2 more minutes. Season with lots of salt and pepper, sprinkle with the parsley, and serve.

VARIATION: If you want to be a little bit more adventurous, adding 2 minced garlic cloves, $\frac{1}{2}$ teaspoon chili powder, and $\frac{1}{2}$ teaspoon cinnamon lends some nice spiciness to the ragout.

Onion Pie with Jarlsberg and Thyme

SERVES 4

IN NORWAY, THIS SIMPLE DISH IS USUALLY MADE WITH JARLSBERG OR GOUDA, BUT I HAVE ALSO MADE IT WITH PARMESAN OR GRUYÈRE.

THIS DISH GOES WELL WITH MEAT OR POULTRY.

2 tablespoons unsalted butter

4 to 5 red onions, cut into ½-inch slices

4 garlic cloves, sliced

1 bay leaf

5 black peppercorns

2 to 3 whole cloves

Fine sea salt

1 sheet puff pastry (thawed if frozen)

1 cup grated Jarlsberg, Gouda, Parmesan, or Gruyère cheese

2 teaspoons fresh thyme leaves

Heat the butter in a large skillet over medium-high heat. Add the onions, garlic, bay leaf, peppercorns, and cloves and reduce the heat to medium-low. Cook for about 20 minutes, or until the onions are soft but not brown. Season with salt to taste.

Preheat the oven to 400°F.

Line a medium-size ovenproof dish with puff pastry. Remove the cloves, peppercorns, and bay leaf from the onions and discard. Place the onions in the dish and add the grated cheese and 1 teaspoon thyme. Bake in the oven on the lowest rack for 15 minutes, or until golden brown. Just before serving, sprinkle on the rest of the thyme.

Chanterelles and Spinach

SERVES 4

½ pound spinach, tough stems removed, thoroughly washed, and patted dry

1 tablespoon olive oil

2 garlic cloves, chopped

2 tablespoons unsalted butter

½ pound chanterelles, trimmed, cleaned, and cut lengthwise in half

2 teaspoons chopped fresh thyme

Fine sea salt and freshly ground black pepper

Preheat the broiler.

Spread the spinach on a large baking sheet. Sprinkle with the olive oil and add half the garlic. Bake in the middle of the oven for 3 to 4 minutes, until the leaves are starting to collapse and a few black patches are starting to appear. Remove from the oven.

In a large skillet, heat the butter over medium-high heat until light brown and bubbling enthusiastically. Add the chanterelles and sauté for 4 to 5 minutes. Reduce the heat to medium, add the remaining garlic and the thyme, and season with salt and pepper. Stir in the spinach, cook for 3 more minutes, and serve.

Green Pea Puree with Asparagus and Scallions

SERVES 4

AN ELEGANT VEGETABLE STARTER OR SIDE DISH, THIS GETS THE MOST OUT OF SWEET GREEN PEAS. IF YOU CAN'T FIND FRESH PEAS, SUBSTITUTE FROZEN PEAS. TIMING IS OF THE ESSENCE WITH THIS RECIPE. IT IS CRUCIAL THAT YOU MAKE THE DISH JUST BEFORE SERVING IT, AND THAT YOU DO NOT OVERCOOK THE VEGETABLES.

2 tablespoons salt

8 asparagus spears, trimmed and cut into 2-inch pieces

4 scallions, trimmed and cut into 2-inch pieces

$1/2$ cup veal or chicken stock

3 cups shelled green peas

3 tablespoons unsalted butter

3 tablespoons coarsely chopped pistachios

1 teaspoon toasted sesame oil

Combine 3 cups water and the salt in a medium pot and bring to a boil over high heat. Add the asparagus and boil for 3 minutes. Add the scallions and cook for 2 more minutes. Drain and rinse the vegetables under cold water to stop the cooking process. Set aside.

In a small saucepan, bring the stock to a boil over medium heat. Add the peas and cook for 4 minutes, or until tender; they will not be completely covered by the stock, so stir a couple of times so they cook evenly. Pour the peas and stock into a food processor or blender and pulse until most of the peas are coarsely chopped. Add 2 tablespoons of the butter and process until you have a smooth puree.

In a small skillet, heat the remaining 1 tablespoon butter over medium heat until frothing but not brown. Sauté the asparagus and scallions for 1 to 2 minutes.

Spoon the puree onto four plates. Sprinkle each plate with the chopped pistachios and drizzle with the sesame oil. Add asparagus and serve.

Asparagus Sautéed in Butter and Mustard

SERVES 4

Serve with good bread so that you
can scoop up all the delicious sauce.

1 pound young asparagus

2 tablespoons unsalted butter

1 tablespoon Dijon mustard

1 tablespoon fresh lemon juice

Freshly ground black pepper

Heat a large skillet over high heat. Add the asparagus
and cook for 1 minute. Reduce the heat to medium
and add the butter. When the butter has started
to brown, add the mustard and lemon juice. Season
generously with pepper. Cook gently for 5 to 7
minutes, turning the asparagus every now and then.
The asparagus should be tender but still firm inside.

Serve immediately.

Green Beans and Peas with Celeriac and Mango

SERVES 6

The combination of green beans, green peas, and celeriac is not uncommon in traditional Norwegian cooking, but the addition of mango is a modern influence. Norway's largest non-European minority is from Pakistan, a country that produces fantastically sweet and juicy mangoes. If Pakistani mangoes are not available, any ripe mango without fibers will do. (Fibers make the flesh difficult to cut.)

1 pound green beans, trimmed

1 1/2 cups shelled green peas

1/2 pound celeriac, peeled and cut into matchstick-size pieces

1/4 cup olive oil

3 tablespoons white wine vinegar

1 tablespoon Dijon mustard

Fine sea salt

Sugar to taste

1 ripe mango, peeled, pitted, and cut into 1/4-inch-wide by 1 1/2-inch-long pieces

Cook the green beans in a medium pot of boiling salted water for 3 minutes. Add the peas and cook for 3 more minutes. Drain and transfer to a bowl. While the vegetables are still hot, add the celeriac and mix well.

In a small bowl, combine the olive oil, vinegar, and mustard. Season with salt and sugar to taste; mix well.

Pour the dressing over the beans and peas and toss. Add the mango, mix gently, and serve.

Broccoli with Capers, Garlic, and Anchovies

SERVES 2

THIS DISH IS GOOD WITH ROAST MEATS AND POULTRY AND FATTY FISH SUCH AS SALMON. FOR A LIGHT MEAL ON ITS OWN, ADD SOME CRISPY BACON OR PANCETTA.

2 stalks broccoli, trimmed

¼ cup olive oil

2 garlic cloves, chopped

6 anchovy fillets, chopped

3 tablespoons capers, rinsed and chopped

2 tablespoons fresh lemon juice

Freshly ground black pepper

Cook the broccoli in a saucepan of lightly salted water for 7 to 9 minutes, until tender but not soft. Drain.

In a large skillet, heat a generous tablespoon of the olive oil over medium-high heat. Cook the garlic for 2 minutes. Reduce the heat to medium and stir in the anchovies, capers, and half the remaining olive oil. Add the broccoli and cook for 2 minutes, turning so that all the florets are dipped into the anchovy oil.

Place the broccoli on plates, and pour the lemon juice and the rest of the oil over it. Season to taste with pepper and serve immediately.

Norwegian canned anchovies, which are actually brisling (a fish in the herring family), are generally much spicier than Italian or Spanish anchovies. When I make this dish in the States, I use Italian anchovies, but you might find it interesting to taste this spicy variety (see Mail-Order Sources, page 294).

Stuffed Cabbage Rolls

SERVES 4

Stuffed grape leaves are an important part of Turkish cuisine. When Swedish king Karl XII, who governed Sweden from 1697 to 1718, spent four years in Turkey, trying to build an alliance with the Turks against the Russian czar Peter the Great, he got to know and love Turkish food. He was particularly fond of this stylish finger food, which he introduced to Swedish high society upon his return.

The dish has slowly been adapted to Swedish conditions: The grape leaves have been replaced with cabbage leaves, pork has been added, and the level of spiciness has been turned down a few degrees.

½ cup salt

12 large cabbage leaves, trimmed, rough stems removed

2 tablespoons unsalted butter

1 onion, finely chopped

1 garlic clove, finely chopped

½ pound ground pork

¼ pound ground beef

½ cup cooked long-grain white rice

½ cup whole milk

½ teaspoon ground fennel

½ teaspoon ground cumin

Fine sea salt and freshly ground black pepper

1 teaspoon vegetable oil

1 tablespoon sugar or maple syrup

Lingonberry preserves (see Mail-Order Sources, page 294) or whole-berry cranberry sauce (optional)

In a large pot, combine 4 quarts water and the salt and bring to a boil over high heat. Place 6 cabbage leaves in the pot, reduce the heat to medium-low, and cook for 3 to 4 minutes, until softened but not limp. Remove and drain on a rack or kitchen towel. Repeat with the remaining cabbage leaves. Cut the leaves lengthwise in half, removing the tough center ribs. (You will now have 24 half cabbage leaves. You will not need all, but some may tear.)

Heat 1 tablespoon of the butter in a large nonstick skillet. Sauté the onion and garlic until golden and soft. Remove from the heat.

In a bowl, combine the ground meats, rice, onion (set the skillet aside), and milk until you have a loose mixture. Season with the fennel, cumin, salt, and pepper.

Place 1 cabbage leaf on a work surface. Place 2 to 3 heaped tablespoons of the meat mixture in the center of the leaf and mold the mixture into a rough cylinder. Fold and roll the cabbage leaf over; tuck the ends of the leaf underneath. Repeat until you have used all the meat mixture.

Preheat the oven to 350°F. Grease a large baking dish with the vegetable oil.

Heat the remaining 1 tablespoon butter in the nonstick skillet. Add 4 to 6 cabbage rolls at a time, sprinkle with a little sugar, and cook until golden, 2 to 3 minutes. Transfer the cabbage rolls to the baking dish. When all the cabbage rolls are sautéed, deglaze the skillet with ½ cup water. Boil until reduced to 2 to 3 tablespoons and pour over the cabbage rolls.

Cover the baking dish and bake the cabbage rolls for 25 minutes. Let cool until just warm to the touch. Serve with the lingonberry preserves if desired.

Brussels Sprouts with Lemon and Parsley

SERVES 4 TO 6

Brussels sprouts have an almost poetic name in Norwegian, *rosenkål,* which literally means "rose cabbage." Up until the 1960s, while cabbage was king of the vegetables, Brussels sprouts were considered a rather sophisticated vegetable, normally served with fine cuts of lamb or game.

By the time I was growing up, though, the aura of refinement had worn off, and I remember with dread the Brussels sprouts served at family gatherings, cooked until almost brown in color. In order to be allowed a second serving of meat and gravy, I had to finish all the Brussels sprouts on my plate. I was never sure whether the trade-off was worth it.

Today, with a wide array of vegetables available in most shops, Brussels sprouts are no longer thought to be fashionable. I consider that a pity, despite my early misgivings. Brussels sprouts can be delicious when they are not overcooked. Sprinkling them with lemon will help keep their color and emphasize the gentle sweetness—making them true to their Norwegian name.

¼ cup salt

1 pound Brussels sprouts, trimmed

½ lemon, cut into quarters

3 tablespoons fresh lemon juice

3 tablespoons olive oil

3 tablespoons finely chopped fresh parsley

1 tablespoon finely chopped fresh dill

Freshly ground black pepper

In a medium pot, combine the salt with 1½ quarts water and bring to a boil over high heat. Add the Brussels sprouts and lemon wedges, reduce the heat to medium, and cook for about 15 minutes, until the sprouts are tender but still firm inside. Check with a fork; you should feel some resistance in the center of the sprouts.

Drain the Brussels sprouts in a colander and rinse for 30 seconds under cold running water to stop the cooking. Discard the lemon wedges.

While the sprouts are still hot, cut them lengthwise in half and place them in a bowl. Add the lemon juice, oil, parsley, and dill, season generously with pepper, and toss. Serve warm.

VARIATION: If you want to be a bit more inventive, add 2 tablespoons drained capers and 4 chopped anchovy fillets.

Savoy Cabbage with Dill Butter and Bacon

SERVES 4

SAVOY CABBAGE HAS A NICE SWEETNESS TO IT THAT IS EMPHASIZED BY A GOOD LUMP OF BUTTER. THE BEST IS HOME-CHURNED SOUR CREAM–BASED BUTTER.

3 tablespoons lightly salted butter, preferably Home-Churned Butter (page 199), at room temperature

1 tablespoon finely chopped fresh dill

¼ cup salt

2 medium Savoy cabbages, cut in half lengthwise

¼ pound bacon, diced

2 teaspoons unsalted butter

Fine sea salt and freshly ground black pepper

In a small bowl, using a fork, mix the butter with the dill. Refrigerate.

Combine 4 quarts water and the salt in a large pot and bring to a boil over high heat. Add the cabbages, reduce the heat to medium, and cook for 8 to 12 minutes, or until the cabbages are tender but still offer some resistance when pricked with a fork.

Meanwhile, fry the bacon in the unsalted butter in a skillet over medium heat for 7 to 9 minutes, or until crisp.

Drain the cabbages well and place on individual plates. Add the dill butter and bacon, season each plate with salt and pepper, and serve.

THIS IS AN EXTREMELY SIMPLE BUT
DELICIOUS WAY TO SERVE FENNEL. WHEN
COOKED IN BOILING WATER, FENNEL
LOSES MUCH OF ITS FLAVOR. SIMPLY
BAKING IT, ON THE OTHER HAND, SEEMS
TO CONCENTRATE THE FLAVORS. IF YOU
WANT TO ADD MORE FLAVOR, YOU CAN
PLACE A FEW SMALL SPRIGS OF FRESH
HERBS OR BAY LEAVES UNDER THE
FENNEL WHILE IT BAKES.

WITH ITS GENTLE LICORICELIKE FLAVOR,
FENNEL IS INTERESTING AND TASTY, AND
IT WORKS WELL WITH BOTH FISH AND MEAT.

Baked Fennel

SERVES 4

**4 large fennel bulbs, trimmed and
cut lengthwise into ⅔-inch slices**

¼ cup fresh lemon juice

¼ cup olive oil

½ teaspoon fine sea salt

Preheat the oven to 325°F.

Place the fennel in a roasting pan or a large baking
dish. Sprinkle with the lemon juice and olive oil and
season with the salt. Bake in the middle of the oven
for 35 minutes.

Turn the heat up to 400°F and cook for 10 more
minutes, or until tender.

L-R Baked Fennel. Oven-Dried Tomatoes, page 240. Cumin-Baked Parsnips with Salmon Roe, page 241.

DRYING THE TOMATOES IN THE OVEN IS
A GOOD WAY TO GET MORE FLAVOR OUT
OF BLAND VARIETIES, THE LONGER YOU
COOK THE TOMATOES, THE STRONGER
THEY WILL TASTE, BUT THEY WILL ALSO
BECOME LESS FIRM.

Oven-Dried Tomatoes

MAKES 1 POUND

Tomatoes are as important in modern Norwegian cooking as in most Mediterranean cuisines. The problem, though, is that the tomato season is very short, from early July to September. The rest of the year we have to rely on imported or greenhouse-grown tomatoes that do not have the same intense flavor as the homegrown ones.

Serve as a side dish with grilled meat or fish.

2 pounds tomatoes, halved crosswise

1 tablespoon fleur de sel or other flaky sea salt or 1$\frac{1}{2}$ teaspoons regular salt

Freshly ground black pepper

2 teaspoons chopped fresh oregano or other herb(s)

Preheat the oven to 250°F (200°F if you have a convection oven).

Place the tomatoes cut side up in a roasting pan. Season with the salt, pepper to taste, and the oregano. Place the tomatoes on the middle oven rack. Prop the oven door slightly ajar, with the handle of a wooden spoon. Leave the tomatoes in the oven for 3 to 4 hours, until they have shrunk by approximately half. The tomatoes will keep, refrigerated, for 3 to 4 days.

Cumin-Baked Parsnips with Salmon Roe

SERVES 4

PARSNIPS BECOME WONDERFULLY SWEET AND DELICIOUS WHEN THEY ARE BAKED WRAPPED IN FOIL. SERVING THEM WITH SALMON ROE MAKES FOR AN ELEGANT STARTER OR SIDE DISH. WITHOUT THE SALMON ROE, THIS IS EXCELLENT WITH ALL KINDS OF MEATS AND FATTY FISH LIKE SALMON.

2 parsnips, peeled and halved

2 teaspoons ground cumin

3 tablespoons lemon juice

3 tablespoons olive oil

2 tablespoons finely chopped fresh parsley

1 small garlic clove

4 to 6 tablespoons salmon roe

Preheat the oven to 350°F.

Place the parsnips in a small baking dish. Sprinkle with the cumin, lemon juice, and 2 tablespoons of the olive oil. Cover with foil and bake for 40 minutes, or until soft and sweet. Let the parsnips cool off until nicely warm.

Meanwhile, with a mortar and pestle or a mini blender, crush or pulse the parsley, garlic, and the remaining 1 tablespoon olive oil until you have a smooth sauce.

Place the parsnips cut side up on plates. Spoon the parsley sauce over the parsnips, add the salmon roe, and serve.

Cumin and its cousin, caraway, have been common in Scandinavia since the thirteenth century, and, for no apparent reason, they have taken turns as the most popular spice. In many ways caraway has won, being the predominant spice in aquavit.

13

BRING ME BERRIES

My interest in food goes back as far as I do: Being hungry is my earliest memory, and the urge to eliminate hunger governed my life. As a small child, I was both greedy and lazy—at least that is what my parents tell me. And as a baby, I didn't really see the point of walking when I could just continue being carried, as I always had.

Then, one fine summer day in 1974, when I was a little more than a year old, my father placed me in front of a row of raspberry bushes and left me there. Sitting down, I could reach maybe one or two of the beautiful red berries. They were sweet and perfectly ripe. I uttered a demanding sound, as if to say, "More berries!" But there was no one there to obey my commands. If I was going to get more of the juicy berries, I had to stand up. I rose to the occasion, so to speak, and picked a few. And once I was standing, I could see more raspberries, big, crimson red, juicy, velvety raspberries, each one sweeter than the next—just a few feet farther away.

I had to choose between my laziness and my hunger. The temptation was too much—hunger won.

When my father peeked around the corner to see how I was doing, he saw me walking to the other side of the bushes as if it were the most natural thing in the world. I held a berry out for him, my face red with juice and full of pride. The berry fell to the ground. I looked and suddenly noticed how far down it was. I stumbled, fell, and started crying. But this time my father didn't have to pick me up. All he had to do was to point and say, "Look, there's another one." And I got up.

The world, it turned out, was packed with good things. But few can compare to the summer weeks, when life revolves around a few raspberry bushes, when you do not even feel guilty for all the things you should have done, the time when nature, in a short burst of energy, hands us the sweetest berries imaginable and people in the coldest country in the world can finally enjoy the reward for all their patience.

Red Berry Pudding with Cream

SERVES 6

DIFFERENT VERSIONS OF THIS PUDDING CAN BE MADE ACCORDING TO THE SEASON, SOMETIMES USING A COMBINATION OF RASPBERRIES AND CURRANTS, SOMETIMES RASPBERRIES AND STRAWBERRIES. COMMON TO ALL VERSIONS IS A THICKENED BERRY PUREE SERVED WITH SLIVERED ALMONDS AND CREAM. I USE A LITTLE BIT OF WHITE WINE AND VANILLA IN MY RECIPE, AND ALTHOUGH SOME TRADITIONALISTS MAY FROWN WHEN I TELL THEM, FEW DO WHEN THEY TASTE THE RESULT.

1½ pounds raspberries

½ pound red currants, stemmed

½ cup dry white wine

2 to 4 tablespoons superfine sugar, or more to taste

½ vanilla bean, split lengthwise in half

2 teaspoons cornstarch or potato starch

1 pound strawberries, hulled and coarsely chopped

¼ cup slivered almonds

½ cup heavy (whipping) cream

Place the raspberries and red currants in a blender or food processor and blend until pureed.

In a stainless steel saucepan, bring the wine to a boil. Add the raspberry and red currant mixture, 2 tablespoons of the sugar, and the vanilla bean. Simmer over low heat for 10 minutes. Add the cornstarch, stir, and gently bring to a boil. The pudding should thicken somewhat but still be rather loose. Add more sugar to taste if necessary. Add the strawberries, bring to a boil, and remove from heat. Transfer to a bowl, cover, and refrigerate for at least 1 hour.

Spoon the pudding into individual bowls. Sprinkle with slivered almonds and serve the cream in a pitcher on the side.

This is a traditional Danish dessert, and although all the Scandinavian languages are closely related, the name of this dish—*rødgrød med fløde*—can really be pronounced only by Danes. In the words of cookbook writer Dale Brown, Danes let the name "slide out of their lips as smoothly as cream from a spoon."

IF THERE IS A NATIONAL SUMMER DESSERT IN NORWAY, IT MUST BE SUMMER BERRIES WITH VANILLA CUSTARD.

THE CUSTARD CAN BE SERVED HOT, WARM, OR COLD. IT WILL KEEP FOR UP TO TWO DAYS IN THE REFRIGERATOR.

Summer Berries with Bay Leaf Custard

SERVES 4 TO 6

My grandmother picks red currants and wild raspberries every summer morning. Then, just before supper, she makes custard, filling the old farmhouse with the maddeningly delicious aromas of berries and vanilla.

Once there was no vanilla to be found in the house, not even poor substitutes like vanilla sugar or vanilla extract. "You think of something to add," my grandmother told me in her warm yet demanding way. After rummaging through the shelves, the only candidates I could find were a few dry bay leaves. Neither of us was all too optimistic about the experiment, but when the custard was done, it was delicious. I find the bay leaf version to be more interesting and complex than the traditional vanilla custard.

Bay leaves are mostly used in savory dishes, but if you crush a bay leaf in your hand, close your eyes, and take a deep breath, you will notice that it has an aromatic sweetness to it, like a pleasant combination of cinnamon, nutmeg, vanilla, and cardamom.

Even though bay leaves keep well when dried, fresh ones have the most intense and complex flavor. If you have a favorite vanilla custard, feel free to stick with that recipe and just replace the vanilla with bay leaves.

5 large egg yolks

1/4 cup superfine sugar

1 cup whole milk

1 1/4 cups heavy (whipping) cream

2 to 3 bay leaves, preferably fresh, plus 4 to 6 for garnish (optional)

2 pounds mixed berries, such as blueberries, strawberries, raspberries, and/or currants, stemmed and/or hulled

In a medium bowl, whisk the egg yolks and sugar together until pale and thick.

In a medium saucepan, combine the egg yolk mixture, milk, cream, and bay leaves. Heat gently over medium-low to low heat, stirring constantly, until the custard thickens enough to leave a velvety coating on the back of a wooden spoon. (If you are using a thermometer, the custard should reach about 175°F.) Do not let the mixture boil or it will curdle. Remove it from the heat as soon as you have obtained the right thickness and continue stirring for 2 more minutes. Leave the bay leaves in the custard while it cools, then remove them.

Place the berries in dishes, pour the custard over, garnish with bay leaves, if desired, and serve.

POLAR BERRIES

In Norway, summer does not merely mean sun and warmth, it is compensation for the long, dark winter, and it is savored hungrily. Even in the capital, Oslo, in the south of the country, the sun does not set until nearly 11 P.M., and it quickly rises again before 4 A.M. In northern Norway, the sun never sets. In June and July, outdoor restaurants and beaches are overcrowded with sun seekers, and after a few long days of sun and temperatures in the eighties, we forget how on a cold, dark day in January we regretted being born in one of the northernmost countries in the world.

The true sign that summer has arrived comes in June, when the first Norwegian strawberries start to appear in shops. Highly regarded by most people, strawberries are seen by Norwegians as the true essence of summer, something few could imagine living without. During Norway's national vacation in July, stalls are put up along all the roads to sell nothing but fresh strawberries.

In June, the first berries from the south-facing slopes of the Lier Valley, close to Oslo, hit the stores.

They are juicy, sweet, and just a little bit tart, best eaten with sugar and cream or as a part of the traditional cream cake. The first strawberries are typically the Zephyr or Honey varieties—followed by Korona and the poetically named Senga Sengana and, toward the end of the season, Bounty and Dania.

As summer progresses, and strawberries from farms farther north start coming in, the berries get sweeter and sweeter. By mid-July, the somewhat smaller berries from Trøndelag, in the middle of the country, are ripe. They hardly need any sugar at all. If they are combined with other fruits or berries, they will seem almost overpowering, and while I am usually skeptical of combining normal strawberries with chocolate, the Trøndelag berries are up to the challenge.

Then, toward the end of July or the beginning of August, the season culminates with the berries from Harstad, north of the Polar Circle, the northern-most commercially grown strawberries in the world (but facing stiff competition from a few Swedish farms almost at the same latitude). If the summer

has been colder than average, the berries will not have had time to ripen at all before the cold northern-Norwegian autumn finishes them off. But in good years, the crimson Harstad berries are a worthy conclusion to summer. Their aroma is almost as intense as wild strawberries', and their flavor is just as wonderful. I have not yet come across a way to serve the berries that makes them better than the way nature—and the ever-present sun—made them.

Strawberry Snow

SERVES 6 TO 8

1 pound strawberries, hulled and halved

½ to 1 cup confectioners' sugar

3 cups heavy (whipping) cream

1 to 2 tablespoons fresh lemon juice, to taste

Combine two-thirds of the strawberries and half the sugar in a blender and puree until smooth. Add more sugar to taste. Press the pureed strawberries through a fine sieve to remove the seeds.

Just before serving, whip the cream in a large bowl until stiff. Coarsely chop the remaining strawberries. Dust the chopped berries with a little sugar and sprinkle with the lemon juice. Gently fold the pureed and chopped strawberries into the cream and serve.

VARIATION: You can make all kinds of variations on this mousse by adding either some vanilla seeds or some finely chopped fresh thyme, basil, or even rosemary to the cream. Or serve in ice cream cones or caramel baskets for a nice, crispy contrast to the smooth mousse.

Wild Blueberry Parfait

SERVES 8 TO 10

A PARFAIT IS PERHAPS NOT "PERFECT," AS ITS FRENCH NAME INDICATES, BUT IT IS A REFRESHING WAY TO CONCLUDE A MEAL. AND MAKING A PARFAIT IS MUCH SIMPLER THAN MAKING EITHER ICE CREAM OR A PROPER FORTIFIED MOUSSE. IT CAN BE PREPARED A DAY IN ADVANCE, BUT IT IS BEST WHEN JUST FROZEN.

3 cups heavy (whipping) cream

2 large egg whites (optional)

5 large egg yolks

2/3 cup superfine sugar

1 1/2 cups wild blueberries, blackberries, or black currants

8 fresh mint leaves, finely chopped

3 tablespoons coarsely grated bittersweet chocolate, or more to taste

In a large bowl, whip the cream until stiff. In a medium bowl, beat the egg whites until stiff. Gently fold the whites into the whipped cream.

In a medium bowl, whisk together the egg yolks and sugar until thick and pale. Whisk in 1 cup of the blueberries and the mint, beating until most, but not all, of the berries burst and the mixture turns dark violet. Fold the blueberry mixture gently into the whipped cream.

Transfer the parfait mixture to a 1 1/2-quart mold, or leave it in the bowl. Cover with plastic and place in the freezer for at least 8 hours.

Forty minutes before serving, transfer the parfait to the refrigerator.

To serve, place the mold in warm water for a few seconds and invert the parfait onto a serving plate. Garnish with the rest of the berries and the chocolate and serve immediately.

Commercially grown blueberries do not have the intense color and flavor of the wild berries, which make this dish interesting to eat and pretty to look at. If you cannot find wild blueberries, substitute blackberries or black currants.

If you are not absolutely sure that your eggs are safe, I suggest you use pasteurized raw egg yolks and omit the raw egg whites.

CLOUDBERRIES: REACH DOWN AND TASTE THE CLOUDS

Cloudberries grow in the Arctic and sub-Arctic areas of the Nordic countries and North America. The berries have a deep red color when nearly fully ripe, then change to golden with a tinge of orange when ripe. Their shape resembles a raspberry, but their flavor is more like deep caramel or baked apples than that of any other berry (the cloudberry variety that grows in Canada and Alaska is often referred to as "baked apple berry")—and, surprisingly, it is not sweet. The long days and cool weather in the highlands give the aromas time to develop, but there is not enough warmth for the berries to produce sugars.

I decided to embark on a quest for the illustrious cloudberry and ended up in Koppang, five hours north of Oslo. I soon learned however, that picking cloudberries is not easy. The low bushes are almost impossible to spot. The first day there, I spent hours head down, bottom up, searching the moors, unable to find more than a pound of the golden berries, most of which I ate as I picked them. The next two days I had better luck, but still I returned to the city with only two 3-quart containers, much less than I had hoped for.

Luckily, just a few cloudberries go a long way— their intense flavor encourages slow savoring. Because they are not sweet, they can be served with game and other meats, but first and foremost, they are used to make cloudberry cream—whipped cream, sugar, and cloudberries combined to make a delicious dessert that is like a cloud wherein all the flavors of the intense Arctic summer are captured.

Cloudberry Cream with Rosemary and Vanilla

SERVES 2-4

BECAUSE THEY ARE SO RARE AND THEIR FLAVOR SO MILD AND EPHEMERAL, CLOUDBERRIES ARE ALWAYS SERVED THE SIMPLEST WAY POSSIBLE, EITHER AS CLOUDBERRY CREAM OR AU NATUREL WITH CREAM AND SUGAR ON THE SIDE. SOME CLOUDBERRY PURITANS WILL PROBABLY THINK MY ADDITION OF A HINT OF ROSEMARY AND VANILLA IS A DANGEROUS EXPERIMENT, BUT I FIND THAT BOTH FLAVORS ADD SOMETHING INTERESTING TO THE BERRIES, WITHOUT BECOMING TOO DOMINANT.

**1 pound cloudberries
or 1 pound cloudberry preserves
(see sidebar)**

**6 tablespoons sugar, or more to
taste, if using fresh berries**

3 cups heavy (whipping) cream

**1 vanilla bean, split lengthwise
in half**

**2 tablespoons finely chopped
fresh rosemary**

If using fresh cloudberries, sugar them to taste. They should be pleasantly sweet but still have a little tartness.

Pour the cream into a large bowl. Scrape the black seeds out of the vanilla bean and add to the cream. Whip the cream until stiff. Fold in the cloudberries and rosemary. Serve immediately.

If you cannot get hold of fresh cloudberries—and, unless you live in the northern United States, where they grow wild, this will likely be the case—you can substitute cloudberry preserves and will probably not need any sugar. If you cannot find cloudberries in a local shop, try ordering them by mail (see Mail-Order Sources, page 294).

Norwegian Pancakes

SERVES 2 TO 4

NORWEGIAN PANCAKES ARE QUITE
DIFFERENT FROM AMERICAN PANCAKES.
THEY ARE NOT LEAVENED AT ALL AND
ARE MORE LIKE A COMBINATION OF
A FRENCH CRÊPE AND A THIN OMELET.
LIKE CRÊPES, THEY CAN BE SERVED
EITHER AS A DESSERT OR AS A SAVORY
DISH. IT ALSO QUITE COMMON TO SERVE
PANCAKES WITH STRAWBERRIES OR
BLUEBERRIES AND SUGAR FOR DINNER.

MY FATHER IS A MASTER PANCAKE MAKER,
AND WHEN I WAS A CHILD, WE HAD
PANCAKES FOR DINNER ONCE A WEEK.

$2/3$ cup all-purpose flour

$1/4$ teaspoon salt

3 large eggs

$1\frac{1}{2}$ cups whole milk

1 tablespoon sugar or honey,
plus more for serving

3 tablespoons unsalted butter,
melted, plus butter for cooking

Blueberries or strawberries
for serving

Combine the flour and salt in a medium bowl.
Add the eggs, milk, and sugar, stirring with a fork
until you have a light batter; make sure there are
no lumps. Stir in the melted butter. Let rest for
30 minutes.

Heat 2 teaspoons butter over medium heat in a
cast-iron or other heavy skillet. Add $1/3$ cup of
the batter and immediately tilt the skillet so that the
batter spreads out evenly. Cook for approximately
3 minutes, until the batter has set on top, then flip,
using a spatula. Cook for 2 minutes, then transfer
to a plate. Repeat, stacking the cooked pancakes,
until you have used all the batter.

Serve the pancakes warm with berries and sugar.

MORE SUGAR, PLEASE!

When I was a child, of all the things the grown-ups ate, two were completely incomprehensible to me: red wine and rhubarb, sour-tasting things that did not even try to please but instead filled your mouth with a nasty, numb dryness. Rhubarb was the worst, since that was the one I was subjected to—every year, as summer approached, I would watch the reddish stalks grow with furious energy, dreading the day the grown-ups would discover them and decide to make a terrible acidic rhubarb soup, almost without sugar, cooked for hours until the rhubarb had disintegrated into a thick pulp.

I would protest, naturally, but it was useless. "You have got to taste it. Maybe you will like it now" was the standard, merciless command. The amount of soup made was enormous, and if it was not finished, which it seldom was, it was recycled as a refreshment. "If the rhubarb hates summer so much, why can't it grow in winter?" I asked. There was no reply.

Today I know that the rhubarb is not to blame. It knows of only one existence, that of an angry, acerbic lust for life. If it is to be enjoyed by humans, it has to be subdued by a staggering amount of sugar. It was not until I wrote a cookbook with restaurateur and chef Sissel Kvello that I tasted a really good rhubarb soup. The soup she made contains white wine, vanilla, and cinnamon, and it is not cooked for hours. Sissel's rhubarb soup is now one of my favorite summer desserts. It is just interestingly tart, quite spicy, and so sweet that you can feel the blood sugar pumping around in your veins—everything my childhood's rhubarb dishes were not.

WHILE RHUBARB IS INCREDIBLY SOUR AND TAKES A POTENTIALLY DIABETES-PROVOKING AMOUNT OF SUGAR TO MAKE IT ENJOYABLE ENOUGH TO EAT, I THINK IT SHOULD BE ALLOWED TO KEEP SOME OF ITS REBEL CREDENTIALS. RHUBARB SOUP SHOULD BE TART AND REFRESHING. ADDING THE SWEET AROMAS OF VANILLA AND CINNAMON WILL ALLOW YOU TO USE SOMEWHAT LESS SUGAR. I PREFER TO USE A DRY WHITE WINE THAT HAS NOT BEEN AGED IN OAK BARRELS, BUT YOU CAN USE ANY DECENT WHITE WINE YOU LIKE.

Rhubarb and Strawberry Soup

SERVES 4

1 pound young rhubarb stalks, trimmed and cut into 1$\frac{1}{2}$-inch pieces

$\frac{1}{2}$ cup sugar, or more to taste

2$\frac{1}{2}$ cups water

1 cup dry white wine

1 vanilla bean, split lengthwise in half

1 small cinnamon stick (approximately 2 inches)

2 teaspoons potato starch or cornstarch (optional)

12 to 16 strawberries, hulled and sliced

1 tablespoon chopped fresh mint

Sour cream for serving (optional)

In a stainless steel pot, combine the rhubarb, sugar, water, white wine, vanilla bean, and cinnamon stick (do not use a copper, iron, or aluminum pot, as they can be discolored by the strong acidity from the rhubarb and may affect the taste of the soup). Bring to a boil over medium-high heat, reduce the heat to medium-low, and simmer gently for 25 minutes, or until the rhubarb is very soft.

Remove the cinnamon and vanilla and discard the cinnamon. Scrape the remaining seeds out of the vanilla bean with the back of a knife and return them to the soup. Discard the bean. If you want the soup to have a somewhat thicker consistency, add the potato starch and bring to a boil. Remove from the heat. Add half the strawberries to the soup and set aside to cool.

Pour the soup into deep bowls, garnish with the mint, the remaining strawberries, and sour cream, if desired, and serve at room temperature or chilled.

A TASTE OF HONEY

"Bees are something you do not understand, Andreas. But when you do, new horizons will open up to you," my grandfather once told me in a rare moment of grandparental conversation. My grandfather was normally a man of few words and even fewer opinions, and I felt tremendously privileged to have been found worthy of his confidence. And he was most certainly right. I did not understand, but I immediately started guessing what his cryptic message could mean. Then, a few moments later, he added, as if to clarify: "You see, bees make honey."

I knew that, did I not? There was nothing mystical about that. At first I was truly disappointed. Was that all there was to my grandfather, was that all the wisdom he hid behind his gloomy and quiet exterior?

Honey is nectar from flowers, gathered by bees and broken down by their saliva. It is as simple as that—yet that cannot be all there is to it. There is a magic surrounding the transformation of plain sweet nectar into golden honey, something that cannot be explained in full by chemists, something only

a lifelong fascination with bees can make familiar, but even then never fully understandable.

I always loved the smell of my grandparents' basement, where my grandfather kept his beekeeper workshop. He would oftentimes let me taste honey straight from the comb. And, in a way that anyone who has had a profound childhood experience of something wonderful will recognize, honey will always mean something special to me. As time has passed, I have learned to appreciate the many different kinds of honey.

The first honey of summer is light and translucent, tasting of apple and raspberry blooms. Later, as summer evolves, the honey develops deeper and more intense flavors. And it also varies from region to region, according to vegetation. When there is a lot of clover and Indian cress (nasturtium), the honey will have a nice spiciness to it. I have friends in Oslo who make their own honey in the middle of town. The bees fly off to gather nectar in parks, gardens, and balcony flower boxes, producing a honey that is the sweet fingerprint of the city.

But the most important honey in Norway, what the country is famous for, is heather honey.

During summer, many beekeepers transport their beehives from their farms to the highlands, where the bees gather the nectar from heather, cloudberry flowers, and other mountain plants. The result is an opaque yellow honey, so thick that it will not pour, and with so much flavor that adding just a teaspoon of it to a cup of tea is enough to fill the whole room with the sweet scent of heather.

I have made many attempts to grasp what my grandfather meant by his cryptic statement, and I think I am beginning to see what he sought in his bees. Perhaps he, like the Belgian author and Nobel laureate Maurice Maeterlinck, saw in the bees a more perfect society, a life with a purpose that could never be questioned. "The bee may not be the world's most intelligent creature, I will not argue with you about that," Maeterlinck wrote in *La Vie des Abeilles (The Life of the Bee)* in 1901. "But the bee has found a way to prevent cold and hunger, death, time, and loneliness, and all those enemies that threaten our own lives. The toil is hard, but the reward is sweet."

When my grandfather dressed in his white beekeeper costume and went out to tend to his small brown and yellow bees, he was fully content. Once I even found him singing to his bees in a frail, rusty voice, while the bees walked peacefully over his old hands. At moments like that, he seemed at peace, with himself and with the world. I believe he admired and envied the small creatures. The bees do not wrangle, they do not talk about insignificant things. They stay where they belong and, most of all, they work. And when fall arrives, and the bee has fulfilled its obligations to the world, it does not sit down to feast. Instead it lies down to die. It is not difficult to see the poetry in that.

Baked Apples with Honey and Ginger

SERVES 4

Ginger, although undeniably a very "exotic" and Eastern spice to many, has been known in Scandinavia at least since the sixteenth century, perhaps as far back as the fourteenth century.

Ginger was originally used for medicinal purposes, but it gradually worked its way into many Scandinavian cakes and desserts.

4 sweet apples, such as Golden Delicious

¼ cup honey

2 tablespoons finely chopped ginger

2 tablespoons unsalted butter

4 teaspoons sour cream, or more (optional)

Preheat the oven to 450°F.

Remove the core from each apple without cutting all the way through, forming a hollow ⅔ inch to 1 inch in diameter. (If you are preparing the apples in advance, brush them with lemon juice to prevent discoloring.) Place the apples in a baking dish. Fill the cavities with the honey and chopped ginger and top each one off with a small lump of butter.

Bake on the lowest oven rack for about 45 minutes, until the apples are tender. Check on the apples every once in a while—if there are signs that the honey is burning, turn down the heat.

Serve hot or warm, topping each apple with a teaspoon or more of the sour cream, if desired.

Baked Apples with Lingonberries

SERVES 4

THIS IS A LOVELY, SLIGHTLY TART DESSERT THAT WILL HELP PICK YOU UP AFTER DINNER. SIMPLE TO MAKE, IT CAN BE PREPARED IN ADVANCE, AND IT CAN BE SERVED WITH NOTHING BUT ITS OWN SYRUPY COOKING JUICES AND, PERHAPS, SOME WHIPPED CREAM.

4 sweet apples, such as Golden Delicious

1 vanilla bean

6 tablespoons superfine sugar

2/3 cup lingonberries or cranberries, halved, or 2/3 cup lingonberry preserves (see sidebar)

Sweetened whipped cream (optional)

Preheat the oven to 400°F.

Remove the core from each apple without cutting all the way through, forming a hollow 2/3 inch to 1 inch in diameter. Remove the peel from the upper quarter of each apple. (If you are preparing the apples in advance, brush them with lemon juice to prevent discoloring.)

Place the apples in a baking dish. Cut the vanilla bean lengthwise in half. Remove the small seeds with the back of a knife and rub the exposed flesh of the apples with the seeds. Dust the flesh with 3 tablespoons of the sugar. Cut the half beans in two and place one in each apple. (The beans will perfume the apples nicely as they cook.) Fill the apples with the lingonberries. There will not be room for all the berries, so scatter the rest of them around the apples in the dish. Top off the berries with the rest of the sugar (if you are using preserves, no more sugar is needed).

Bake on the lowest oven rack for 45 minutes, or until tender, spooning the cooking juices over the apples once or twice. Serve warm, with whipped cream, if desired. Remove the vanilla bean before eating.

The lingonberry is a northern European relative of the cranberry, smaller and more sour than the cultivated American cranberry, but not unlike the wild variety. Both berries derive their names from similar—and equally dubious—assumptions: The cranberry was long thought to have been the favorite food of cranes, and the lingonberry was said to have been preferred by cows, *lingon* in Swedish. You can buy frozen lingonberries and lingonberry preserves in Scandinavian specialty stores or by mail (see Mail-Order Sources, page 294), or substitute cranberries. If you are using sugared lingonberry preserves, reduce the sugar to 1/4 cup.

I made this dish on the *New Scandinavian Cooking* program from Lofoten in northern Norway, where it was so cold that some of the lingonberries on the plate froze, while the apples were still scorching hot inside.

Cream Cake with Rosemary Pears and Strawberries

SERVES 8 TO 10

In an American book on Scandinavian food from the 1960s, Norwegian cream cake is dismissed as "a cake consisting almost exclusively of cream." This is not exactly a misstatement, but it shows a deep lack of understanding. Whereas a cheesecake or chocolate cake, for example, is supposed to be heavy and full of flavor, the cream cake is featherlight, fresh, and festive. Cream cake is normally served on May 17, Norway's constitution day, and at birthday parties, weddings, and other special occasions.

FOR THE SPONGE CAKE

1 teaspoon unsalted butter

4 large eggs, separated

1 cup superfine sugar

1 cup all-purpose flour

2 teaspoons baking powder

FOR THE FILLING

1 vanilla bean, split lengthwise in half

One 15-ounce can pears in light syrup, drained, syrup reserved

1 tablespoon finely chopped fresh rosemary

4 cups heavy (whipping) cream

$\frac{1}{2}$ cup superfine sugar, or more to taste

1 pound strawberries, hulled

2 tablespoons Calvados or eau-de-vie (optional)

$\frac{1}{4}$ cup strawberry or orange juice (optional)

Preheat the oven to 350°F. Grease a 10-inch nonstick round cake pan or springform pan with the butter.

To make the sponge cake, beat the egg whites in a large bowl until stiff peaks form. In another large bowl, beat the egg yolks and sugar together until pale and thick. Sift together the flour and baking powder, and beat into the egg mixture. Fold in the beaten egg whites as gently as possible. Pour the batter into the prepared pan.

Bake in the middle of the oven for 30 to 35 minutes, until a toothpick inserted in the center comes out clean. Let the cake rest for 10 minutes before you remove it from the pan, then let it cool completely on a rack.

To make the filling, scrape the seeds from the vanilla bean with the back of a knife, and reserve for later. Cut the pears into thin slices. Set aside a few of the nicest slices for decoration (brush them with lemon juice to prevent discoloring).

In a nonstick skillet, combine the rest of the pears, the vanilla bean (not the seeds), and the rosemary and cook over medium heat for 5 minutes, or until the pears start to lightly brown. (If the pears dry out completely, add a little of the reserved syrup.) Remove the vanilla bean and discard. Set aside to cool.

Whip the cream in a large bowl until stiff. Add the sugar. Transfer approximately one-third of the cream to two small bowls, dividing it evenly.

Reserve 8 of the nicest strawberries for decoration. Puree two-thirds of the remaining berries in a blender, or push them through a sieve using the back of a spoon. Coarsely chop the rest of the berries and mix with the puree in a bowl. Gently fold the strawberry mixture into one of the small batches of whipped cream. If necessary, add more sugar to taste, but the mixture should still have some gentle tartness left.

Stir the vanilla seeds into the other small batch of whipped cream.

With a long, thin knife, cut the cake into three layers. Place the bottom layer of the cake on a large serving plate. Soak the cake with some of the syrup from the pears. Sprinkle with the Calvados, if using. Arrange the pears on top. Spread the vanilla cream over the pears. Add the second layer of sponge cake. Soak the cake with strawberry juice, if using. Spread the strawberry cream over the layer. Place the final layer on top. Frost the entire cake with a thick layer of cream. Decorate the cake with the reserved strawberries and slices of pears. Serve immediately.

Veiled Farm Girls

SERVES 4

This is a traditional dessert that both Norway and Denmark lay claim to. Given our colonial history, though—Norway was subject to Denmark's rule for nearly four hundred years—there is reason to believe that the Danes invented the dish.

How it got its name is easy to understand: It consists of layers of applesauce and sweet cinnamon-scented bread crumbs, veiled with whipped cream.

1½ cups bread crumbs

3 tablespoons superfine sugar

2 teaspoons ground cinnamon

2 tablespoons unsalted butter

1½ cups heavy (whipping) cream

1½ cups applesauce, chilled

½ cup chopped hazelnuts

In a nonstick skillet, combine the bread crumbs, sugar, cinnamon, and butter. Stirring constantly with a heatproof spatula or wooden spoon, heat over medium heat until the crumbs are uniformly golden. Remove from the heat.

In a large bowl, whip the cream until stiff.

Layer the applesauce, bread crumbs, and cream in individual glass bowls. (I prefer at least two layers of each.) The top layer should always be whipped cream, "veiling" the dish. Sprinkle with the chopped nuts and serve.

L▸R Veiled Farm Girls. Aquavit Sorbet, page 277.

Pears with Ginger, Juniper Berries, and Caraway Cream

SERVES 4

JUNIPER BERRIES ARE IMPORTANT IN SCANDINAVIAN COOKING, BUT USING THEM IN DESSERTS IS NOT COMMON. I PREPARED THIS DESSERT WHILE WE WERE IN SVALBARD TAPING *NEW SCANDINAVIAN COOKING.* I FOUND THAT THE SPICES LENT AN INTERESTING LAYER OF FLAVORS AND AROMAS TO THE GENTLE AND UNCOMPLICATED PEAR. WITH THE WARM SWEETNESS OF HONEY AND THE CLEAN SPICINESS OF GINGER, THIS DEVELOPED INTO A DELICIOUS AND UNEXPECTED DESSERT.

1/4 cup honey, preferably heather honey

1 tablespoon unsalted butter

4 pears, such as Anjou, peeled

2 tablespoons finely chopped ginger

8 juniper berries, ground or finely crushed

1/4 teaspoon chili powder

1/2 cup heavy (whipping) cream

1 teaspoon caraway seeds, crushed

1 tablespoon aquavit (optional)

1 tablespoon superfine sugar

In a large nonstick skillet, heat the honey and butter until a dark caramel starts to form in the center of the pan. Immediately reduce the heat and add the pears, ginger, juniper berries, and chili powder. Cook the pears, turning them every few minutes, for 20 minutes over medium-low heat, or until tender but still somewhat firm near the core. Remove from the heat.

Whip the cream in a small bowl until stiff. Fold in the caraway seeds, aquavit, if using, and sugar.

Place the pears on plates and spoon the honey caramel sauce over, followed by the whipped cream. Serve immediately.

Aquavit Sorbet

SERVES 6 TO 8

THE SPICY CARAWAY FLAVOR OF AQUAVIT IS NOT WHAT MOST PEOPLE ASSOCIATE WITH A DESSERT, BUT WHEN MIXED WITH SUGAR, AQUAVIT MAKES A VERY INTERESTING AND REFRESHING SORBET. IF YOU REDUCE THE SUGAR BY HALF, THIS CAN ALSO BE SERVED AS A PALATE CLEANSER BETWEEN COURSES.

1 cup superfine sugar

2 tablespoons finely grated lemon zest

2½ cups water

¼ cup fresh lemon juice

⅔ cup aquavit

In a small saucepan, combine the sugar, lemon zest, and water and bring to boil over high heat. Boil over medium heat for 5 minutes. Add the lemon juice and set aside to cool.

Strain the syrup into a bowl. Add the aquavit and place the bowl in the freezer. Take out and stir energetically with a fork every 30 minutes until completely frozen.

If the sorbet is frozen hard, let it soften briefly in the refrigerator before serving.

Serve with fruits or lightly toasted slivered almonds.

Crunchy Almond Brittle Ice Cream

MAKES 1 1/2 QUARTS

This is the traditional Scandinavian ice cream. There are related ice creams with nougat in France and Italy, but I have not tasted anything like the deliciously crunchy *krokanis,* as it is called in Norwegian.

Serve with fresh strawberries, if you like.

FOR THE ICE CREAM

2 1/2 cups whole milk

1 1/2 cups heavy (whipping) cream

1 vanilla bean, split lengthwise in half

10 large egg yolks

1 cup sugar, plus more to taste

FOR THE ALMOND BRITTLE

2/3 cup sugar

1 tablespoon unsalted butter

1/2 cup slivered almonds

2 tablespoons chopped hazelnuts

To make the ice cream, combine the milk and cream in a large saucepan. Scrape out the small black seeds from the vanilla bean and add both the bean and seeds. Heat until almost boiling. Keep hot over low heat, stirring occasionally.

In a large bowl, whisk together the egg yolks and sugar until thick and pale. Little by little, add the hot milk and cream mixture, whisking constantly. The mixture should thicken into a smooth, thick custard that leaves a thick film on the back of a spoon; if the custard is still too thin, return it to the pan and heat, whisking continuously, until thickened (it should reach about 175°F on a candy or instant-read thermometer). Do not overheat or the custard will curdle. Let the custard cool until lukewarm, then chill in the refrigerator (or freezer) until very cold.

Freeze in an ice cream machine according to the manufacturer's instructions, transfer to an airtight container, and freeze. Or, if you do not have an ice cream machine, transfer the custard to a container with a tight-fitting lid and place the container in the freezer. Take the custard out every 20 minutes and stir it with a spatula, making sure to scrape the frozen crystals from the sides of the container, until the ice cream is frozen and it gets difficult to move the spatula around. Return to the freezer.

To make the almond brittle, cover a table with parchment paper. Heat a large nonstick skillet over medium-high heat. Add the sugar and butter and cook until the sugar has melted and you have a golden brown caramel. Add the almonds and hazelnuts, stirring to coat. Immediately pour the caramel onto the parchment paper and spread it out with a spatula until ¼ inch thick. Let cool.

Coarsely chop the almond brittle. Mix most of the almond brittle into the ice cream and return it to the freezer until ready to serve. Reserve the remaining almond brittle for garnish.

14

SKÅL!

"Skål!" (Pronounced "scawl.")

This toast has, since at least the Viking age, been a symbol of friendship, respect, and togetherness, and any visitor to Scandinavia will be surprised at how frequently the friendly word is uttered. But it does not take long to discover that the amiable encouragement to drink up has a long and apparent history. In the Viking sagas, a man who did not drink up his horn when a toast was presented was seen as unreliable. Knowing how to drink, that is, to get as drunk as your drinking companions, neither much more nor less, was a quality just as highly regarded by the Vikings as strength, honesty, and brutality.

Luckily, our societies have progressed considerably since the time when the fearless and cruel Vikings terrorized the good people of Europe. Our thirst has also diminished considerably. But Scandinavians are still social drinkers, and to a not-so-thirsty stranger, the social aspect may feel like something in between friendliness and coercion.

As recently as the nineteenth century, a dinner party in rural Sweden could include as many as seven toasts: a "welcome toast" as the guests arrived (and more than one if the guests arrived in several groups), an "appetite toast" as the party was seated, a "fish toast" with the fish, a "meat toast," a "pancake toast" with dessert, a "give thanks for the food toast," and a "farewell toast." If even more toasts were exchanged over the table, a dinner party could be quite excruciating, at least for a stranger lacking the stamina of his or her Scandinavian hosts. The only thing not allowed, if there were more than five people at the table, was toasting the hostess. Drunkenness was more a rule than an exception, and in order to have some control over the situation, the hostess had to be excused from the mandatory drinking.

What you drink helps determine how you are drinking, and the aquavit, snaps, and beer culture of Scandinavia may explain why we love to toast. Going back in history, the mead and beer made by the Vikings was so weak that great quantities had to be drunk before any effect could be felt. At the other extreme, neither aquavit—spiced and cask-aged potato liquor—nor snaps—spiced or herb-infused grain spirits— is meant to be savored. Unlike wine, which should be sniffed, sipped, and enjoyed as slowly as possible, aquavit or snaps should be tossed back quickly, the warm sensation you feel afterward being almost as important as the flavor.

There is an old saying that "the Danes live to eat, the Norwegians eat to live, and the Swedes eat to drink." While Danes traditionally enjoyed eating rich food, and Norwegians struggled to survive, Swedes developed a rich culture of spiced spirits, easy homemade alternatives to the expensive aquavit, whose production was normally controlled by the aristocracy or clergy. In 1756, Sweden had more than 180,000 registered home distilleries, one for every ten Swedes. Today snaps is one of the most important aspects of the Swedish gastronomic heritage, a tradition that is continually expanded to include new, more exotic flavors like lemongrass and kumquat.

Snaps and aquavit were seen as something in between medicine and alcohol, and even people who claim they do not drink have been known to take the occasional sip of aquavit to "help arthritis" or snaps to "clear a sore throat," "alleviate indigestion," or "improve circulation." Assigning different medicinal qualities to different types of snaps is partly a continuation of the traditional herbal medicine, partly an excuse for drinking.

Making your own snaps is an easy way to turn plain vodka into something interesting. If the liquor you are using as a starting point is good and quite neutral in its flavor, the process is very easy: Just put something spicy or tasty that you like—be it parsley, lemon zest, coriander seeds, chile peppers, rose petals, or ginger—into a couple cups of liquor and let it stand for a few days. The alcohol will draw flavor, and sometimes color, out of the spices, leaving the various types you make not only different tasting, but also different looking. I think I like the process of making snaps as much as drinking it—seeing how the spirits start to change color and sipping a small sample of each every evening to ascertain whether it is done or needs one more day before I can remove the spices and place it in a bottle with a homemade label.

The Devil's Rhubarb

SERVES 4

THIS IS RHUBARB FOR THE HARDENED
RHUBARB LOVER, STALKS OF RHUBARB
DIPPED IN SUGAR AND SERVED WITH
VODKA. A SOUR COMPANION FOR SUNNY
DAYS, A PREDINNER DRINK, OR SOMETHING
TO WAKE YOU UP AFTER A HEAVY MEAL—
THE KIND OF SNACK/DRINK THAT WILL
MAKE YOUR MOUTH SORE YET STILL
LONGING FOR MORE.

**8 thin stalks very young
rhubarb, trimmed**

1/2 cup sugar

2/3 cup very cold vodka

Peel the rhubarb so that only the juicy interior
remains.

Place the sugar in a small bowl. Dip the rhubarb
in the sugar and take small bites. Clean your mouth
with sips of vodka from small glasses.

IF YOU LIKE THE DIFFERENT SORTS OF
LEMON-FLAVORED VODKA ON THE MARKET,
YOU WILL DEFINITELY LIKE THIS SNAPS.
ONLY THE ZEST IS USED FOR FLAVORING,
SO YOU SHOULD MAKE SURE THAT YOU
USE A GOOD ORGANIC LEMON.

EXACTLY HOW LONG THE SNAPS SHOULD
BE ALLOWED TO STAND BEFORE THE
SPIRITS HAVE ENOUGH FLAVOR DEPENDS
ON THE TEMPERATURE AND, OF COURSE,
ON HOW SPICY YOU PREFER IT TO BE.

Lemon Snaps
with Coriander

MAKES 1 LITER

One 1-liter bottle grain vodka

1 lemon, washed

1 tablespoon coriander seeds

Pour the vodka into a glass jar. With a sharp knife or potato peeler, remove the colored zest from the lemon. Add lemon zest and coriander seeds to the vodka and close the jar tightly. Let stand at room temperature for 2 to 4 days, depending on how much flavor you want and how intense the aromatic oils in the lemon zest are. If you want to speed up the process, place the jar in a sunny window.

While the snaps is macerating, wash off the label from the original bottle and replace with a homemade label.

Strain the snaps and pour back into the bottle. Add a few of the coriander seeds to the bottle for decorative purposes. Serve in shot glasses.

OTHER GOOD EASY-TO-MAKE SNAPS

SNAPS WITH DILL: Add 1 small bunch fresh dill to a bottle of vodka. Let stand for 1 to 2 days.

SNAPS WITH GINGER: Add a 1$\frac{1}{2}$-inch piece of ginger, cut into slices, to a bottle of vodka. Let stand for 2 to 4 days. Strain out the ginger before serving.

SNAPS WITH CINNAMON AND CARDAMOM: Add 1 cinnamon stick and 2 cardamom pods to a bottle of vodka. Leave the spices in the vodka indefinitely.

SNAPS WITH HORSERADISH: Add 3 tablespoons coarsely chopped horseradish to a bottle of vodka. Let stand for 12 to 24 hours. Strain out the horseradish before serving.

SNAPS WITH MINT: Add 1 small bunch mint (2 ounces) to a bottle of vodka. Let stand for 2 days.

SNAPS WITH BLUEBERRIES AND CINNAMON: Add $\frac{1}{3}$ cup wild blueberries and $\frac{1}{2}$ cinnamon stick to a bottle of vodka. Let stand for 2 days before straining out the blueberries; the cinnamon can be left in the vodka indefinitely or until you find the cinnamon flavoring overpowering.

SNAPS WITH LEMONGRASS AND STAR ANISE: Add 2 stalks trimmed lemongrass, 3 star anise, and 4 black peppercorns to a bottle of vodka. The spices can be left in indefinitely or until you find the flavoring overpowering.

Mulled Wine

MAKES 1 QUART

This is the traditional drink that is normally served at pre-Christmas parties, when days are at their darkest and people really need something uplifting. In the traditional drink—*gløgg* in Norwegian—it is normal to add a generous amount of vodka to the hot wine, but I find that too overpowering and, frankly, too intoxicating.

1 cup water

3 to 4 tablespoons honey or sugar

1 stick cinnamon

4 whole cloves

4 cardamom seeds

One 750-ml bottle red wine

½ orange, sliced

In a medium pot, combine the water, honey, cinnamon, cloves, and cardamom, and bring to boil. Simmer over medium-low heat for 2 to 3 minutes. Pour half the syrup into a separate bowl, being careful not to pour out any spices. Add the red wine to the pot containing the spices and remaining syrup. Heat over medium-low heat until the temperature is about 170°F on an instant-read thermometer. Remove from heat and add the orange slices. Add the reserved syrup to taste. Serve warm.

THE WATER OF LIFE

Aquavit is the national drink of Norway, and undoubtedly the most important drink in the whole of Scandinavia. No traditional Scandinavian meat-rich meal should be served without a little digestive help from a small glass or two of the heavily spiced potato or grain liquor.

Aquavit dates back at least to 1531, when the archbishop of Trondheim received a bottle of liquor along with a letter stating, "I send Your Grace some water called *Aqua vitae.* This water cures all types of internal diseases from which a human being may suffer." Its name, of Latin origin, means "water of life," and at first it was hailed as a remedy for everything from labor pains and rheumatism to indigestion, headaches, colds, gangrene, and lice. Lumbermen were supplied with bottles of aquavit in order to keep warm and to have something to drink that would not freeze while they worked in the forest, and farm workers would have a glass or two in the morning before they went out to the fields. After a while, the authorities realized that aquavit too had its limitations and started discouraging its use and levying taxes

on it like other alcoholic beverages. But by then it was a part of the national character, and versions were made in tens of thousands of home distilleries— a tradition that is still practiced today.

Although its name points to a close relationship with other "waters of life," like the French eau-de-vie and Scottish-Irish whiskey (whose original name, *usquebaugh,* also means "water of life"), aquavit seems to have developed into something uniquely Scandinavian. The Norwegian versions are made from potato liquor, but in Sweden and Denmark they may be also made from grain liquor. Most are heavily flavored with caraway, dill seeds, and fennel, some with anise, coriander, cumin, lemon zest, wormwood, or cinnamon. Certain varieties are aged in oak casks; others are served young and raw.

I enjoy a cold shot of well-made aquavit with traditional foods, especially around Christmas, and as something warming after a long ski trip. I am, however, forced to admit that I prefer the aquavit I make myself to the store-bought variety. Only then do I have full control over all the flavors.

Mock Aquavit

MAKES 1 LITER

IT MAY NOT ALWAYS BE SO EASY TO FIND AQUAVIT IN LIQUOR STORES IN THE UNITED STATES. ALTHOUGH THERE ARE MANY FINE COMMERCIALLY MADE AQUAVITS, I ACTUALLY PREFER HOMEMADE "MOCK" AQUAVIT. ONLY THEN DO I HAVE THE OPPORTUNITY TO EXPERIMENT WITH ALL THE FLAVORS I LIKE: ANISEED, ANGELICA, WORMWOOD, JUNIPER, LEMON ZEST, CURLED MINT, ETC.

2 teaspoons caraway seeds, or more

1 teaspoon fennel seeds

2 teaspoons dill seeds

2 star anise

1 tablespoon coriander seeds

1 whole clove

One 1-inch cinnamon stick (optional)

2 teaspoons cumin seeds (optional)

One 1-liter bottle potato vodka

Add the spices to the vodka bottle and cover tightly. Let stand for 2 to 3 weeks, depending on how strong you want the aquavit to be. Shake the bottle every once in a while.

When the aquavit has reached the desired intensity of flavor, strain and discard the solids; return the aquavit to the bottle.

MAIL-ORDER SOURCES

D'ARTAGNAN
www.dartagnan.com
Specializes in game and poultry (including goose and grouse), with a wide selection of wild mushrooms as well.

DEAN & DELUCA
www.deananddeluca.com
Offers delicacies of all kinds, including stockfish (bacalao).

FAMILY FARMS
www.familyfarms-direct.com
Offers a good selection of fresh food, including seafood.

GIFTS OF NORWAY
www.giftsofnorway.com
Offers books, souvenirs, and a limited selection of food, including cloudberry preserves.

LARSEN'S BAKERY
www.larsensbakery.com
A Seattle bakery specializing in Scandinavian products.

LOUISIANA CRAWFISH COMPANY
www.lacrawfish.com
Offers crawfish shipped directly from the farm to your door.

MRS. OLSON'S LEFSE
www.mrsolsonslefse.com
Offers lefse and a few other Scandinavian specialties.

NORDIC HOUSE
www.nordichouse.com
Offers a wide selection of Scandinavian foods, including selected cheeses and frozen foods.

THE NORTHERNER
www.northerner.com
Offers a wide selection of Scandinavian foods, including aquavit, cloudberry preserves, and reindeer products.

SCANDIA BAKE SHOP
www.scandiabakeshop.com
Minneapolis's oldest Scandinavian bakery.

SWEDEN'S BEST
www.swedensbest.com
Offers a limited selection of Swedish specialties, including lingonberries.

WIKSTROMS' GOURMET
www.wikstromsgourmet.com
Offers Scandinavian delicacies, including fish products.

ACKNOWLEDGMENTS

There are so many people I want to thank—those who have been instrumental in one way or another in helping give birth to *Kitchen of Light.* I must ask forgiveness from anyone whom I may have left out.

I would first like to thank my good friend Andrea Clurfeld for convincing me that it was possible for me to write this book and have it published in the United States, and Jim Eber at Workman Publishing for his help and encouragement while the book was still just an idea. And I would like to thank my agent, Lisa Ekus, and her staff for their hard work and enthusiasm. "You're the top...."

I would also like to thank everyone at Artisan for their skills in making the book, especially Ann Bramson, my publisher, for believing in it; Pamela Cannon, my editor, for her comments, humor, and insistence that there is always room for improvement; and Vivian Ghazarian for making the book so beautiful. Thanks also to Deborah Weiss Geline, Judith Sutton, Nancy Murray, Amy Corley, Emma Straub, and Barbara Peragine.

Thank you to my foodie friends Jeffrey Steingarten and Herve This for inspirational conversations, Scott McKay for useful comments on the recipes, and Sally King for testing the food.

My family and friends in Norway gave me great support and inspiration. Thank you to all, especially my grandparents and parents for teaching me that everything is possible.

Thank you to my partners at Nett-tv: my producers, Anders Sæther, Morten Ottesen, and Alexander Wisting, for making the series *New Scandinavian Cooking with Andreas Viestad* a reality; and the crew, Kaare Skard, Angela Amorosa, Knut Kollandsrud, Erik Røed, Monica Viken, Lotte Vikant, and Merete Steen, for making all the traveling and work so much fun. And thanks to all the people we met along the way, especially Ola Aukrust, Lars Tyssebotn, Conrad Johansen, and Leif Kristiansen. Thank you, too, to everyone at American Public Television in Boston and Wellspring in New York.

I would also like to thank my editors at my newspaper, *Dagbladet,* for being so understanding: John Olav Egeland, Gunnar Bleness, Hege Duckert, Jo Randen, and Lillian Vambheim.

Thanks to Magnus Castracane and Henrik Henriksen for their help in styling the food for photography.

And finally, thanks to Mette Randem for being such a fantastic photographer, and being so inspiring to work with year after year.

beet(s):
   salad, prune-stuffed pork meatballs
       with, 194–95
   soup with goose stock, Svalbard, 18
Bergen, 23–24, 54
Bergen fish soup, 26–27
Berhardsen, Terje, 145–46
berry(ies), 245–46, 250–51
   in Norwegian pancakes, 258
   red, pudding with cream, 247
   summer, with bay leaf custard, 248
   see also specific berries
blueberry(ies):
   parfait, wild, 255
   snaps with cinnamon and, 287
Bocuse d'Or, 10, 120–21, 211
bouillabaisse, 25
"Brassica Napus" (Døving), 197
brisling, 231
broccoli with capers, garlic, and
       anchovies, 231
Brown, Dale, 247
Butler, Carl, 163
butter:
   home-churned, 199
   and mustard, asparagus sautéed in,
       228
   parsley, poached pollock with, 117
   rosemary-lemon, herbed halibut
       with, 100–101
   Sandefjord sauce, cod with liver,
       roe and, 63
   in tarragon lobster with asparagus,
       147

C

cabbage:
   lamb in, 157
   and lamb stew, 158
   red, compote, glazed duck with
       orange sauce and, 214–15
   rolls, stuffed, 232–33
cake, cream, with rosemary pears and
       strawberries, 272–73
Canada, 256
canapés of smoked salmon,
       asparagus, and potato cake, 47
capers, broccoli with garlic, anchovies
       and, 231
caraway cream, pears with ginger,
       juniper berries and, 276
cardamom:
   snaps with cinnamon and, 287
   veal glace, scallops with celeriac
       puree and, 138
carpaccio:
   salmon, with lingonberries, 49
   scallop, 137
Catholic Church, 64
cauliflower soup with chervil, frothy, 31
celeriac:
   in Bergen fish soup, 26
   in goose stock for Svalbard beet
       soup, 18
   green beans and peas with mango
       and, 230
   puree, scallops with cardamom veal
       glace and, 138
   in traditional vegetable beef soup,
       20

chanterelle(s), 219–20
   crispy mackerel with, 106
   new potatoes with dill and, 79
   and spinach, 224
   squab with pistachios, potatoes
       and, 213
   see also mushrooms, wild
cheese:
   brown goat, 177–79
   brown goat cheese sauce, juniper-
       spiced venison with, 181
   Gruyère, in potato gratin with
       parsnips and rutabaga, 72
   Jarlsberg, onion pie with thyme
       and, 223
   Parmesan, crab cakes with parsley,
       mustard and, 151
chervil:
   frothy cauliflower soup with, 31
   mayonnaise, salt-baked salmon
       with, 92
chicken:
   roast dill-scented, with leeks and
       potatoes, 208–9
   with saffron and cinnamon, 210
chile(s):
   in bacalao stew, 67
   parsley-steamed pollock with
       mussels, clams and, 119
   white wine–steamed crayfish with
       garlic, coriander and, 143
chili glaze, sweet, grilled mackerel
       with charred sage and, 107
chocolate, 251
   in wild blueberry parfait, 255

Christmas dishes, 186–99
   aquavit-flambéed pork loin chops
       with apple and onion compote,
       196
   breast of goose with apples,
       prunes, and port reduction,
       192–93
   home-churned butter, 199
   mashed rutabaga, 198
   pork rib roast with cloves, 190–91
   prune-stuffed pork meatballs with
       beet salad, 194–95
cinnamon:
   chicken with saffron and, 210
   snaps with blueberries and, 287
   snaps with cardamom and, 287
   thyme-and-garlic-steamed mussels
       with, 132
clambakes, 100
clams, parsley-steamed pollock with
       chile, mussels and, 119
cloudberry(ies), 256
   cream, 257
   cream with rosemary and vanilla,
       257
clover, 265
cloves, pork rib roast with, 190–91
cod, 53, 54, 55–68, 188
   bacalao stew, 67
   with liver, roe, and Sandefjord
       butter sauce, 63
   pan-seared, with garlic potato
       puree, 60
   roe with bay leaf and cucumber
       salad, 62
   rosemary, with vanilla-scented
       mashed rutabaga, 57

Published by Artisan
A Division of Workman Publishing, Inc.
708 Broadway
New York, New York 10003-9555
www.artisanbooks.com

Library of Congress Cataloging-in-Publication Data

Viestad, Andreas.
    Kitchen of light : new Scandinavian cooking with
    Andreas Viestad / by Andreas Viestad.
        p. cm.
    Includes index.
    ISBN 1-57965-216-6
        1. Cookery, Scandinavian. I. Title

    TX722.A1 V34 2003
    641.5948—dc21   2002038441

Printed in Singapore
10   9   8   7   6   5   4   3   2   1

Book design by Vivian Ghazarian

This book was set in Akzidenz Grotesk